Half Pass Six

The Arcturus Expedition, 1925

Barbara Lockhart

SECANT PUBLISHING

Secant Publishing LLC
615 North Pinehurst Avenue
Salisbury MD 21801 USA

www.secantpublishing.com

ISBN 979-8-9989611-1-3 (hardcover)
ISBN 979-8-9989611-0-6 (paperback)
ISBN 979-8-9903562-9-0 (ebook)

Except as otherwise noted, photographs of the *Arcturus* and its voyage are taken from *The Arcturus Adventure*, 1926, authored by William Beebe.

Dedicated to the memory of William Beebe
1877-1962

But the ocean yields to nothing in its grandeur, in its age, in its ceaseless movement and the question remains forever unanswered, “Who shall sound the mysteries of the sea?”
William Beebe, *The Log of the Sun*

"My absorption in the mystery and meaning of the sea have been stimulated and the writing of this book aided by the friendship and encouragement of William Beebe"
Rachel Carson, *The Sea Around Us*

Dedicated to the memory of my dad,
William H. Rohrbein
1909–1966

Weary of myself, and sick of asking
What am I, and what I ought to be,
At the vessel's prow I stand, which bears me
Forwards, forwards, o'er the starlit sea.

"Self-Dependence," by Matthew Arnold

Contents

Stardust

The night drew them into its silence, the air still, the water calm and placid as the moon cast its light across it. Two figures stood on the third deck of the ship a few yards apart, elbows on the deck rail, a tall, thin, balding man and the other, a teenager who was careful to make no sound. They were as unlike in physical presence and stature as they were in social aspects, unknown to each other but together now through mere happenstance. It was just the two of them leaning, watching, taking in the strange light on the surface of the water, which appeared as though it had been sprinkled by some ancestral spirit. The lights might be individual or not, but they were great in number, mysteriously infinitesimal and myriad as stardust.

For the moment, in this captivating visual, they owned the night and the mystery before them while others slept, the crew, the professors, the artists, the photographers, those who mended the nets, all of them sleeping with the gentle rocking of the ship. The boy had come to watch the man while the man stared oblivious to anything but the surrounding light near the surface of the water.

Suddenly, the man left the railing and with long, hurried strides headed to the upper deck. He soon came back carrying a net, a quart preserve jar, and a rope which he tied to the net with his long nimble fingers. He plunged the net, now containing the jar, into the sea. He leaned far over the railing, watching that the net and the jar did not descend to any depth as he held one end of the rope, while the boy, watching his every movement in the semidarkness, hoped the man wouldn't lose his balance when he leaned so far. The boy only knew this man as the boss man, Herr Beebe, the one who he heard was famous, the one who had secured the ship and all its purposeful, specialized apparatus to journey toward adventures in the Atlantic and Pacific Oceans to find out what lived in the deep seas of his dreams. The ship was the *Arcturus*, formerly a luxurious yacht, now equipped for exploration.

The boy only understood boats and fishermen heading out from Bremerhaven to find the best places to catch fish, fish that would fill the markets each day, fresh and slippery, smelling the way he thought the ocean must smell. But to simply look at fish and wonder about them was something else. If they couldn't eat them, what good would that do?

Soon after the war, the British blockade prevented the Bremerhaven ships from sailing out of the harbor. Then there were not even enough fish to go around and soon after that, the crops of potatoes failed and there were only long lines for bread and for turnips. *Mutter* said the turnips came from Sweden where the people had taken pity on them. For a long time, there had been only turnips. It's not that he hated turnips although they would never be something he would choose, but the memory of that time of turnips and his empty belly and thin arms would come back to haunt him.

Day after day, since they left New York Harbor, he'd watched Herr Beebe whenever he could, from hiding places where he wouldn't be seen as he kept a vigil of his own until he was needed in the galley. As far as he could see, it must be a great curiosity that drove Herr Beebe. It was what men could do if they didn't have to labor in the train yards laying and repairing the tracks like his father did, worrying about supplying food for their family or paying the rent from meager earnings or being called into the army. The workmen he saw in Bremerhaven kept the wheels of the world rolling. He'd never imagined there was something else, something beyond what an ordinary man could do. But Herr Beebe was no ordinary man, he could see that. Beebe looked ordinary with his strange hat, his torn khaki pants gaping open at the knees and his habit of moving quickly as he leaped about in canvas shoes. What was extraordinary was his excitement after a day pulling up and emptying the nets and finding things so small they had to be put under a microscope to be seen. He was at it again. As soon as Herr Beebe pulled up the net with the jar, he rushed to the laboratory on the top deck.

The chances of the boy, Willi Rohrbein, just sixteen years old, being on this ship in the year 1925, were as phenomenal as the sight of stardust on the ocean. He'd been a stowaway from Germany and was put out to sea on an American ship as soon as he'd arrived in Brooklyn. Because he was illegal, he couldn't stay, of course, confirmed by his mother's nervousness about visitors to the apartment in Brooklyn. He was fortunate to have a job now so he could pay his way, even though no pay was offered since he boarded the ship. He was paid in other ways, because hired as a mess boy he was never hungry, a problem that was the only constant in his young life. His childhood had been consumed by war and hunger and when the war was over, there was still hunger.

William Beebe, on the other hand, was well educated, an explorer and a scientist from the time when he first roamed the wilds of New Jersey lowlands at the age of twelve. It was an obsession from the Victorian era when such activities were popular. Everyone was encouraged to pursue and fill drawers and vessels with what became their prized collections. It was a childhood of freedom and observation that was carefully and tirelessly recorded by young Will, as his parents called him. It was the beginning of his life's work, elicited by his insatiable curiosity. There were no limits for William Beebe. He'd never been hungry except for another day exploring the Jersey wilds.

Drawn together along the railing of the *Arcturus* that night, the experience of the light scattered on the surface of the sea had the same effect on them both. There was a stunned silence broken now by the pulling up of the water-filled jar and the man's haste toward the laboratory where he would put the collection of sea life under a microscope and spend hours late in the night counting the number of creatures in the jar while the boy crept to his bunk alongside the galley and waited for the first rays of the sun.

In the laboratory, Beebe recorded an unseemly number of 271,080 copepods: shrimp, many varieties of snails, egg masses of snails and creatures yet to be named. Collectively, these organisms made up what is called plankton. They carried their own illumination but there was no use mentioning this to the boy with whom he shared the deck that night. The word *bio-luminescence* would be beyond the boy's ability to understand as he spoke very little English. But Beebe was aware of the boy watching everything. He could be seen hiding on the other side of the lifeboats and on the steps to the decks and would turn up on deck at the sound of the captain's horn or the winches pulling in the nets as if he was part of the crew which he was, technically, but on the lowest rung of it all, watching, watching. Beebe respected the boy's curiosity, yet he wondered about the boy's furtiveness and suspected it was fear. The boy's name was Willi.

Worlds apart, they happened to be on the same ship, and they shared the same first name, William.

Willi from Bremerhaven

He was ten years old when the Great War ended. Winters in Bremerhaven came early and were always cold and sullen with a dank and endless wind that blew in from the North Sea, bringing with it the smell of salt water and oil and smoke, where ships crowded the harbor, always coming and going. But the winter of 1916, when he was seven years old, was especially cruel, ruining any crops that might have been, causing the severe rationing of food. The grey and red-brown buildings and streets of stone stood shy of any personality. There was sameness everywhere except for the huge railyard where his father worked. By 1918, the emigration center through which crowds gathered, clutching valises and carpet bags filled with meager belongings, meant crowded city docks and streets. A ragged bunch. At times, it felt like all of Europe was leaving. Everyone but him. He was as ragged as the rest of them.

There was no sun in Bremerhaven. Always it hid behind the drape of blanketing, steely grey clouds. The world was a pale and windy and cruel place. He was always cold. The too-short sleeves on his jacket were not enough. Nothing was ever enough. The iced cobblestones on the streets, the icicles hanging off the buildings, the icy brass doorknob on the old oak door, the empty fireplace, the wet and sometimes stiff sheets hanging across the room and in the attic, too, where his mother washed and waited for them to dry so she could iron them for those who could afford it, and the cold oatmeal, the lack of a sweater—it all made him anxious. He never said a word about it. None of them did. This was their punishment—losing the war, losing territory, the return of Alsace-Lorraine to France, reparations not paid, supplies cut off, the resulting poverty and shame. Was it like this the world over? Was he wrong to dream of warmth and light somewhere instead of failure? All this sadness and shivering? Lessons in school still clung to what was: a country that was Europe's strongest economic and military power. But four long years of war and Germany was in ruins. The fragile Weimar Republic couldn't hold on to territory, lost all its colonies and a tenth of its population. The printing of more money resulted in hyperinflation, wiping out the value of savings and the mark. Despair was everywhere. People walked with their heads down.

As he did. Lips pulled in, teeth clenched, squinting, the muscles in his cheeks bulging with intensity, and the emptiness in his belly. Their constant fight against uncertainty. By age nine, it was innate. The natural order of things. He kept all of it under his skin while he longed for warmth and food and a place like a house with heat, and money enough so his mother wouldn't have to take in washing. But he didn't see how anything would ever change. He would spend the rest of his life chasing something he knew was there though not how he would get it. In his nine-year-old mind, he imagined some sort of magic.

It was a shameful story he could never tell. He vowed to keep it under his skin, as he returned to the moment when he pushed open the old, clattering oak door to the apartment on Olin Strasse, where he lived with his mother, Christine, and his sister, Lieschen, and listened to the heavy bang and rattle of the door shutting behind him. His father used to live with them on Olin Strasse, too, but he was hardly ever home, so it never felt like his father really lived there. When he was little, he remembered watching his father dressing well after work at the train yard. ("A dandy," *Mutter* said with a certain bitterness, "and handsome," she noted with an element of pride.) He could be seen walking in the park with his friends. His name was William Augustus Rohrbein. Drafted, he had to go to war. Now he wasn't working at his job or walking with his friends, nor had he worked for a long time at anything. It was the war from which Germany hadn't recovered that made his mother put her hands on her hips and bear the worry lines imprinted on her otherwise smooth complexion. The effects of the mustard gas were not always detected right away, they were told. His father's injury could not be seen except for the blisters in his nose and throat, but when the hemorrhaging began, it could not be stopped. It was not a missing arm or leg, or a head wound like the neighbor, Carl, came home with, but with each hemorrhage from his lungs, his father grew weaker. They might have to take out a lung, *Mutter* said. He never heard his father speak of war or his injuries when they visited him in the rest home, but his silence hung over the very air they all breathed. William Augustus was in Heidehaus, a sanitarium for wounded soldiers. He'd been there for almost a year. As though he was afraid to move, he lay very still.

One time, Lieschen was standing in the kitchen when he got home from school, while *Mutter*, who probably had spent the morning gathering laundry from those who were better off and from the nursing home as well, was likely working in the attic of their apartment building washing and hanging the sheets in the damp cold. Taller than him and a year younger, Lieschen pushed her fiery, riotous red hair away from her face and bent to light the stove with a long stick match and waited. With her hands on her hips, she eyed him as her mouth broke into a smile. "*Villi, essen*," she said as she pushed a plate of turnips at him. You would have thought she was the older one by the way she took charge. She was not shy, and he was, being small for his age with a wayward eye that suggested confusion and unseemliness of manner. That defeated, frightened look stayed with him when he looked in the windows of the storefronts to see if he still existed. Tears came when he heard Lieschen say, "She had to go to the Heidehaus. Papa is bad again." The momentousness of it. The strangeness that wouldn't go away.

The laundry piled high and with the snow and rain and cold, the task of washing and drying became impossible, even as the apartment house attic was filled with sheets hanging from the rope lines that were tied to the beams. Lieschen and he tried to help after school, but it was never enough. *Mutter* came home and worked far into the night to catch up.

But this day was different. She came home with a pillowcase covered with blood. Just the pillowcase, dry now and neatly folded over her arm. He knew what it was without a word being spoken. The hemorrhaging couldn't be stopped. After a long struggle, his father, William Augustus Rohrbein, had died that afternoon. And his mother, Christine Nordhauson Rohrbein, would save that stained pillowcase for the rest of her life.

Although it was late in the day with the darkness of winter already descending, *Mutter* told Lieschen to run to the other side of the city to inform her sister Bertha of William Augustus's death. She chose Lieschen, not Willi, to run into the dark winter night across the city alone. He would have gone despite the boys who teased him at school and bullied him in the afternoons as he was walking home. Despite the times he got beaten up. He was small for his age, thin and bony as many of the kids were, but he was easy prey, the one with the wandering eye. Lieschen was slightly taller, stronger, faster, and more practical. Lieschen would run the errand in the night, unafraid and daring. The message was clear. He was the weaker one. Or was it the unspoken message that women took care of everything, an education sent down through the ages by mothers? Some things women had no control over, but problems they could always fix, actions they would always accomplish with quiet determination if not without complaint. It was some kind of ancient wisdom passed down through the ages, although the final word was always from the men. Women, then, were often caught in a storm, wallowing. Waiting for a word.

The cost of his father's burial depleted any savings *Mutter* might have had. A simple wooden cross for now, but a small garden over the grave was started. It was a statement of a caring, loving family, a family of little means who could bury the father with dignity despite the makeshift wooden cross. *Mutter* tried to put aside money for the memorial stone, but it would take years. Still, to be buried with pride was something. The garden let everyone know the family Rohrbein did not put a father in a pauper's grave. It was the only recourse to pretentiousness, toward unspoken and assumed gentility despite their condition, their pride in the middle of a lost war and a lost society. Tradition was to be followed. It was the only thing left. Meanwhile, the queues at the soup kitchens grew longer, and he would be sent to wait from early in the morning till late afternoon, while his mother did the laundry with her lips tucked, underlining a heart filled with bitterness.

Soon after, the worry over Father lifted, both his scarce presence, *Wo ist Vater*?, and his worrisome illness and absence as he stayed for a year in Heidehaus. Otherwise, everything was the same.

The long lines of people with promises and hope and satchels kept leaving Germany right through the port of Bremerhaven, the largest and busiest port in Europe, while Lieschen and *Mutter* and he stayed and stayed in a country ravaged by war, stayed in Bremerhaven where people (seven million of them from 1870 to 1974) followed the dream right out of the harbor to flee the devastation and hard times, while across the ocean...who knew? A farm in the country maybe, a boarding house in the Catskills where rich people left the city for vacations in the mountains. Warm fireplaces with plenty of wood and stoves filled with coal. His parents often talked about it, but nothing ever came of it. Plans took money.

He remembered when the potatoes ran out and when the men and horses were called up during the war. Bread made from potato flour, (*K-Brot* or *Karoffeln*), had to be rationed.

His mother used corn, lentils, and even sawdust to make bread. Then the food riots happened. Soon everything was rationed.

THEN ONE DAY AS spring brought birdsong to the trees, there was Tante Anna, his father's sister. She came bustling in from America as if blown in by the gales of the North Sea, her long hair tied up in a braid that wound around her head, round and round, with no end in sight. He wondered how long her hair really was. She was a *heftig,* broad-shouldered woman, thick in the waist as a man who liked his beer. A take charge matriarchal woman of no nonsense, with her own song to sing. America hadn't changed her much, had maybe accentuated this quality where she was not inhibited by the lack of money. Her husband, Helmut Pyttlik, made good. They were the envy of all the relatives who would ever after associate going to America with an accumulation of wealth and prosperity. How Tante Anna and Uncle Helmut made their way in America so well was a mystery no one knew the answer to except *Mutter* said Uncle Helmut was involved in shipping and the Pyttlik Shipping Company was a successful enterprise during and after the war when people and goods poured in and out of American harbors. Shipping goods was foremost in the Pyttlik line, not passengers. Ellis Island was avoided, which is why Helmut could make a few extra dollars when he sometimes shipped a person or two along with the goods.

Tante Anna told stories about how Helmut was against the unions in America. "They vill kill us," she said, a bit of prophecy she could never have guessed, "alvays vanting better pay, better dis, better dat," but Uncle Helmut held fast to his money and his ways. It cost him his life in '34, when the angered union leaders were trying to organize the longshoremen. They finally had enough and beat him up, killing him, but now in 1922, he was king. However, what those relatives who remained in Germany all knew and felt was that both Anna and Helmut had deep ties to family and even now, midst the squalor of the Rohrbeins, Anna Pyttlik visited them in Bremerhaven in the months after her brother-in-law's funeral. "To pay my respects," she said, but they all knew that without a word being said about it, she would help. There was more to her visit than paying respects.

She took charge immediately. There followed a recurring stream of her plans. "A good time to leave. The mark worthless. The *kinder* hungry. Your savings gone. *Nein*. You must get out. To say nothing of vat's happening with Social Democrats, Communists and Nazis planning God knows vat. Germany is ruined!"

In the end, Uncle Helmut paid for Christine's passage on regular transport. The *President Fillmore* was a familiar sight in the harbor at Bremerhaven. It would bring her to Ellis Island, and she could enter the country legally. But Helmut did not offer passage for Lieschen or Willi, that is, until Christine found a job and a place to live and got some money together. Tante Anna's plans continued: "We send Villi to the country, to his grandfather on his father's side. He'll like it there on the farm. And Lieschen vill go to his grandmother, our *Mutter*. Just until you find work and save money for their tickets. *Verstehen?* Understand?"

Then everything happened so quickly. It was rumored that there would be new restrictions on immigrants. America must be kept American. There were numbers now, quotas limiting immigrants, and news of stricter laws that would soon be put in place, laws that were bound to be passed in 1924 in the American Congress. Better to act quickly.

Mutter was gone a few weeks after Tante Anna left. And he, the soon-to-be boy without family, did not even get to see her off. Then Lieschen was on the train. He would have given anything to be with her. He imagined her red hair flying in the wind and her constant waving from the train window. Then, a little while later, he sat on a farm wagon drawn by two black horses into a mist that erased all sense of direction and markers and sound. There was nothing ahead, nothing that he could see, nothing familiar, until they pulled up to a building that loomed up from the ground like a blemish on the landscape. Of grey stone, it was half barn and half house. There was the strong smell of manure and shouts coming from within the house, the lowing of cattle at the other end and the driver of the farm wagon ordering him in a commanding voice to get out now. He was delivered. He was orphaned and he belonged nowhere. He was a child of the war, of uncertainty, abandoned, hungry, poorly clothed and cold.

After Papa died, there was only Lieschen and me and Mutter, and soon after, there was only me.

AS FOR CHRISTINE'S STORY, when the last of the linens had been returned to her customers, she made arrangements for Lieschen to go to her *Grossmutter* by train to the inner city of Hamburg and for Willi to go to his father's father on a small farm on the outskirts of Geestemunde. *Mutter* didn't want her children to see her off on the day of her voyage. She probably didn't think she could bear the sight of them waving from the pier, their bereft faces straining to be hopeful for a future with her in America. No. She would have them whisked away, their thoughts busy with the trip ahead of them and minds temporarily absorbed in what would hopefully be an adventure with extended family.

Willi pictured her on the deck of the *President Fillmore* in the grey wind, so alone now without her husband. They had always planned to go to the Catskills that Anna and Helmut talked about, but now her singularity was probably all she could think about. She was young. William Augustus should be with her. She thought, *Now I am a "come over."* It would be a way to begin conversation when she got to America. People would always ask, "When did you come over?" They were coming from everywhere with so many languages strange to her ears. Happily, most were German. She could talk with them. Already they drew together, commenting to each other about the strangeness of the others, the way they dressed and spoke. Really, they were all alike, she said years later. They were breaking into smiles and laughing and singing when the *Fillmore* pulled into the New York harbor and the sight of the Statue of Liberty drew near.

She soon found work cleaning houses for the New York fortunate. Tante Anna knew people, and while she'd made no effort to become more American in her speech, she could wrangle opportunities and promises out of anyone. Christine lived with the

Pyttliks and worked wherever Tante Anna sent her. Meanwhile the savings account was growing. The children hoped she would send for them soon.

Finally, there was enough for Lieschen's passage. *Mutter* said she couldn't decide whether or not to wait until she had enough for passage for both of them. Lieschen was beautiful, and so young, and coming aboard ship alone in steerage would be a frightening thing, a danger for a young girl alone, so *Mutter* decided to spend her money on first class passage for Lieschen. Willi could wait. She couldn't afford for them both to come, but she could make sure passage for Lieschen was safe. In later years, Lieschen deeply regretted the fact that *Mutter* spent so much money on her ticket and left her brother in Germany. She'd felt guilty about it all her life. She often talked about it to her brother.

But after Lieschen's "come over," *Mutter* received a letter from *Grossmutter*, who had made a visit to the farm where Willi was staying. The letter was about the conditions she saw at his grandfather's that were much worse than she expected. He was treated like a servant as well as a farm hand with barn duties that occupied him day and night. He worked constantly. To say nothing of the beatings if he didn't do a good enough job, which it seemed he never did, according to his grandfather. But it was when *Mutter* read *Grossmutter*'s letter about the lack of food (it was not to be wasted on the newcomer) and the newspapers wrapped around his feet because his shoes were worn through, bruises on his arms and face—the year of unnecessary cruelty sickened her. She thought it explained a lot about her husband, William Augustus, the sudden anger and vengeful aspect of his demeanor. *Mutter* told him later she'd thought it was the war and bad luck, but could this explain his great anger, this unbearable harshness carried over to become a way of life? Men believing a cold, stern aspect would make a man out of a son?

Now was the time to ask for a favor. A very big one. Helmut was not easily approached busy as he was and preoccupied with the shipping business and the longshoremen—the union men who were always demanding their rights and threatening to strike. An act of American laziness, he supposed. They were lucky to be working!

Christine vowed to pay Helmut back every penny. She would sign papers to make it certain and give him some money every week. He didn't answer right away. Then, a few weeks later came the offer. He would get Willi over on the shipping line as a stowaway and it wouldn't cost her a penny. He would be illegal, but Helmut would put him to work on the ships immediately. He didn't need citizenship right away. It was a story told year after year at family gatherings. *Mutter* always imitated Helmut as she was telling it, the words spoken in a whisper as though it was a secret she still had to keep. And her white hair told how long she'd been keeping it. Willi was glad to hear it. For a long time, he'd thought Lieschen was given first passage because she was the favorite, and he was a son who didn't really live up to expectations. He worked all his life to gain favor. Mothers and fathers of his time and station would never concede that some encouragement to offspring would be a good thing. Self-esteem maybe is not something that is given but only earned. Although a little bit of encouragement would have helped. Still, he was not bitter. The name of the game was Survival. He was well equipped to survive, especially when a way opened to him. He reveled in it. He could make his own way.

With those words from Uncle Helmut, his fate was sealed. At the time he had no idea it would be a streak of good luck. He was glad to leave the grandfather whom he feared. Although he was just sixteen, maybe his life was taking shape, maybe bad times and hunger were over. However, the bottom line to all of that was the constant nagging, ice-cold fear that filled his thin bones.

As he stood on the dock in the bitter cold wind, he didn't know the name of the captain who came for him. He was sure it was the captain because the man had on a hat that was adorned with a gold braid. The afternoon sun was just setting, and the winter dusk would be brief. The farmer grandfather had driven off at top speed leaving him standing near the bulkhead with no luggage, just standing there bareheaded in the wind with his white arms hanging way below the cuffs of his sleeves, his hands red and his fingers cracked from the cold. He tried to smile as the captain hugged him quickly and whispered, "William Rohrbein?" and kissed him on both cheeks as though he were a relative. And then another man who was dressed in work clothes came for him and asked him in a booming voice if he'd like to see the boiler room on the ship. "*Yah? Sehr gut,*" as though he was announcing it to the world. The captain trailed behind them.

Instead of the boiler room, he was taken to the captain's cabin, told to sit and wait, that *Kaffee* would come in a little while. That's all he could remember years later, except that he stayed in that cabin for the duration of the trip, with crusts of bread appearing regularly and an occasional *Suppe* when he could tolerate it. Mostly he just lay on the cot next to the wall of the cabin with his eyes shut and his arm over his face, seasick. The captain didn't talk much. Whether he didn't want anyone to hear them, or was just tired, Willi couldn't guess. He did not realize the captain could only speak a few words of German.

After seven days or so (he wasn't sure he was right since day and night ran together and he'd mostly slept), he heard footsteps, men running and shouting on deck and several hoots that were loud enough for him to have to cover his ears as the ship pulled into New York Harbor. The captain came to tell him they would be docking sometime that night.

"Statue?" Willi asked. And since what the captain probably heard was shtaatooeh, he shook his head, and pointing to the floor, said, "Stay here."

He would have loved to have seen it, the famous statue in the harbor, but what he didn't know then was that he would have many chances to see it in the years to come. He waited in the dark, a bit frightened when he thought of how the next part of the journey would work out—if he'd be caught and arrested, maybe sent back to Germany, and excited, too, because it was, after all, an adventure, wasn't it? And his family was waiting. Lieschen would be there and *Mutter*. There was nothing to decide, only to follow with blind faith.

He watched the clock on the wall and waited for dark, or when he thought dark would come. Soon. Soon.

When the captain burst in, his face red and eyes glaring as though he wondered suddenly at the chance he'd taken to smuggle this kid into the country and the thing he'd worried about for all of the crossing was exactly what was about to happen or not happen, his angst grew into anger. All was quiet on deck. The ship would be unloaded in the morning. For now, the captain threw his own jacket over Willi's shoulders and whisked him to the gangplank which had been set in place for the morning's unloading.

Waiting on the pier was a tall, husky man carrying a coat over his arm and smoking a cigar. The smell of it was comforting and in a strange way welcoming. He remembered his father smoking one once when Uncle Helmut visited from America when he was very young. The cigar odor was familiar which was why he thought this man might be Uncle Helmut, but he wasn't sure, and for a moment wished he was going to be in the arms of his father, an occasion that never happened in all his young life. But as the man approached the captain and nodded, he pulled the overcoat from his arm and giving the captain back his jacket, whispered "*Danke*" into the dark, and draped the coat over Willi. Then his uncle took him where the lights burned bright and the streets grew narrow and glowed with the late douse of rain, where brick buildings passed by the trolley window in a blur. He was lost in this big city, still hoping this was his uncle and chose to think it was him (Who else could it be? The man had called him *Villi* like his *Mutter* did and leaning over, said in German, *Wir sind heir.)* They were in Brooklyn now and soon he would be in his new home. In America. *Ja*!

An enormous entrance way and marble steps with an iron railing like the one in Bremerhaven up to the second floor, a knock on the door under the number that said 2-D in gold letters, and then the burst of gladness, which was as short-lived and as intermittent as the streetlights. It was but a moment of family. He wasn't sure what ties there were anymore. *Mutter* had abandoned him and had chosen his sister over him, which he thought he should have understood but now a rawness rose in his throat as he pondered why—when they could have come together and he could have protected Lieschen. But there was Lieschen. Dear Lieschen.

He couldn't stay. That much was plain. *Mutter* cleaned houses. She and Lieschen had papers, but he was illegal. He could be caught, sent to jail, sent back to Germany. They would all live in fear because of it. Uncle Helmut said not to worry. He would find a job out at sea for him. "Give me just a few days," he said, and went out the door, replacing his hat on his head and turning up his collar against the cold. For once, Willi was not cold. The heat in the upstairs apartment was plentiful. Oh, how he wished he could stay.

A few weeks later, Uncle Helmut returned, stomping into the small foyer of their apartment with bluster only a man dealing with longshoremen could muster. In his booming voice he announced that he'd gotten a job for Willi—a job for six, eight months maybe.

His heart sank. There was enough to eat in apartment 2-D and it was warm enough. Sometimes he cleaned with *Mutter* when she went to one of the fancy houses, and sometimes they played cards at night. It was so American, he thought. And he was never hungry. He was even beginning to understand some English. But still, he knew he would have to work. The prospect of months or years out at sea—who knew what that meant? Helmut spoke in English this time, ever so loudly, saying that Willi was to go with him the following morning to see the ship. "It's not so big, but it is a gut ship. You pack your tings, ja? Dey gonna call you de mess boy. You know vat dat iss?"

Willi, not understanding the words, shook his head.

"You make de *Zuppe!*" and he laughed, his burst of deep-throated guttural good-naturedness filling the room. He'd done something good for this lad, this scrawny kid for whom life would not be easy.

William Beebe, Explorer and Naturalist

In previous centuries, there lived many in the world who were curious about what lay beneath and on and inside the earth, in the secrets that lie in ocean depths and in the vast array and variety of living things. Their interest in paleontology and archaeology revealed how the earth sustains life, leaving an unending desire for exploration of the depths of what cannot be easily seen, how the balance in the world is complete in itself before our intrusion at so great a cost and of course, the idea and search for knowledge as to how living things, people, and wildlife, evolved and developed over time. Those individuals, such as Alexander von Humboldt, Charles Darwin, William Beebe, and many others who were instilled with an eagerness to explore, were celebrated in the society of the 1800s and early 1900s.

America was in love with the idea of flight fostered by Lindbergh, in the flight of Piccard in his balloon and the explorations of the poles with men like Peary, Amundsen, Shackleton, and Byrd, but it was William Beebe who explored the ocean depths, an exploration that was new and exciting and especially daring.

The man was not afraid of anything even as he plunged into the darkest, most human life-threatening habitat to reveal ocean secrets and importance in the flow of life. He was pursuing a new vision, the profound interdependence of all living organisms in their natural settings, no matter how rare, obscure, or tiny they might appear. While seeking and finding abundant evidence supporting Darwin's theory of evolution, he was also helping to establish the arena of science that today we know as ecology. This was the insight and proof that Beebe brought to the world, that creatures unknown at the time might link fossils to present life, to reveal how evolution took place, and how present generations are linked to a magnificent chain of events. In Beebe's eight decades devoted to his career as naturalist, explorer and writer, he wrote twenty-four books, among them, *The Log of the Sun* (1906), *Jungle Days* (1923), *The Arcturus Adventure* (1926), and *Beneath Tropic Seas* (1928). He also wrote essays and articles for venues like *Scribner's, The Atlantic Monthly, The National Geographic*, and numerous articles for *The New York Times.* The combination of Beebe's intrepid science explorations and his literary talent to express his findings in poetic prose that anyone could understand formed the basis for his popularity among the reading public.

Born in 1877, Beebe spent his childhood immersed in observations of nature. He was encouraged by his mother, Nettie, and his father, Charles, who had a keen interest in nature and fostered that passion in their only son, Charles William, whom they called Will. Nettie's family was from Glens Falls in upstate New York, and after marriage, Nettie and Charles moved to Brooklyn, where Will was born. To Nettie, brought up in the mountainous wilds of upstate New York, Brooklyn was stifling. Subsequently, Charles moved the family outside New York City to East Orange, New Jersey, where there was easy access to the wonders of the city, while the intrigues of New Jersey's marshes and meadows plus an excellent school system provided a childhood environment suitable for their son. To collect, label, name genres, and share collections of birds and bugs was very much a part of a child's education. To be a naturalist even at a young age was encouraged. It was accessible to anyone.

A key element in William Beebe's education was the fact that Charles, still working in upstate New York even as the family lived in New Jersey, was away from home much of the time, resulting in a close association between father and son. Daily letters to each other regarding what they each had observed in the natural world around them in the mountains of upstate New York and the New Jersey marshes fostered the habit of recording events in language that was attuned to settings, personality, detail, expression and impressions. The pen-to-paper aspect of the father/son relationship was key to William Beebe's ability to write so well of that which filled his days. And write he did, and in doing so, he popularized the theories and evidence of evolution in the oceans as well as lands all over the globe.

The same year Beebe was born, the American Museum of Natural History opened in New York City. It acted as the guardian of the nation's riches and collections from all over the world. Throughout his childhood, Nettie brought the young Will to the museum's Saturday lectures by famous scientists. Botany was a keen interest of hers. She was trained as a teacher of natural history. She also instructed Will in music (he could play mandolin, violin, guitar and banjo). Remembrances of her own childhood in the Adirondacks and letters from Charles in Glens Falls filled with descriptions of hunting and fishing and the birds he had seen, plus the interests of their son in collecting, labeling, and preserving specimens, focused family discussions on the natural world and laid the foundation for their son's life's work. It happened that the young Beebe's enthusiasm and zeal in studying bugs and beetles and later, birds, was something the powers that be in the American Museum of Natural History were well aware of.

At the age of fifteen, Beebe had already decided that he would be both ornithologist and entomologist. He was adept at shooting birds for stuffing and preserving and making notes on the habits and habitats of beetles. His collection was quite sizable as he roamed the woods of the Poconos on summer vacations with his family. It was a time of exploration into the natural world that anyone could accomplish as well as any child who was free to roam the woods and collect birds' eggs and beetles to their heart's content.

At fifteen, he writes:

> *I am tired from my tramps today, and no wonder, for I have been hunter, fisherman, ornithologist, entomologist, conchologist, & taxidermist, & feel I have been fairly successful in each position* (*The Remarkable Life of William Beebe* 27).

It was during those early years that Beebe became devoted to the idea that being a naturalist was the most exciting of callings. He became adept at keeping meticulous records of the life and habits of birds and bugs, at preserving animals, along with making copious notes that eventually turned into volumes. In the last line in Volume III of his careful notes written in 1893, when he was just sixteen, the young Beebe wrote, *To be a Naturalist is better than to be a King* (*Remarkable Life* 26).

In his study of birds, Beebe not only recorded species and preserved them, but he also began dissecting them to find out their unique structure.

> *When we examine the eye of our bird, we see a sense organ of a very high order. Bright, intelligent, full-circled, of great size compared to the bulk of the skull, protected by three complete eyelids* (*The Log of the Sun* 183).

As early as 1906, when Beebe was nineteen years old, a collection of some of his early writings about his explorations had already been published in venues such as *Outing*, *Recreation*, *The Golden Age*, *The New York Evening* Post, and the *New York Tribune*. His book, *The Log of the Sun*, is dedicated to *Mother and Father, whose encouragement and sympathy gave impetus and purpose to a boy's love of nature*. Although the book records numerous observations about birds, insects, and small animals, there is also a chapter on *Secrets of the Ocean*, in which Beebe says, "*But the ocean yields to nothing in its grandeur, in its age, in its ceaseless movement, and the question remains forever unanswered, Who shall sound the mysteries of the sea?" (Log of the Sun* 139*).* It must be said that the idea of oceanic exploration began in Beebe's exploration jaunts on Jersey shores and marshes while he had no idea that he would be the first to explore the ocean a half mile down in a steel bathysphere twenty years later.

During the Victorian period, collections were part of the repertoire of those who could afford to explore the still pristine wild places of the natural world. The influence of people like Teddy Roosevelt and John Muir set the tone and added to the flavor. Old and young alike collected and showed off their specimens, traded ideas and information, all toward the acquisition of knowledge by observation. But Beebe's thinking went beyond that. He was beginning to see how all of life was connected and how each living thing existed in relation to another. This demanded a deeper look than was heretofore explored.

At Columbia University, Beebe was excused from entrance exams and from many other exams because of his outstanding academic and practical achievements. He was also put in advance placement. His collections had extended from bugs and beetles to birds. He had examined the skins of 158 species. He could skin twenty-five birds in Columbia's collection in a day, he told one of his professors, Henry Osborne. It didn't hurt that the head of the Zoology Department, Osborne, was also the president of the Natural History Museum and head of the New York Zoological Society. Beebe's expertise did not go unnoticed. He was invited to give a talk on "Birds in General," which he concluded by playing the mandolin to the delight of the audience who enjoyed his grace and confidence. Osborne then invited Beebe to apply for a job working with birds at the new Bronx Zoo.

THE OPENING OF A ZOO was spearheaded by Theodore Roosevelt and his gathering of ten men of similar interest. They founded the New York Zoological Society, formally established by law in 1895. Roosevelt was aware of the young Beebe, whose reputation as a scientist and writer was growing. He read the articles Beebe had written and mutual admiration grew. When the Bronx Zoological Park opened in 1899, Beebe walked through the iron gates as the new assistant curator of birds. The park, still in the early stages of development, held 843 animals of 157 species. At the opening were the former vice president and governor of New York, Levi Norton; the staff of the American Museum of Natural History; and the zoo's important donors, Percy Pyne, J. Pierpont Morgan, William Dodge, and William Whitney. The aquatic bird area was their first stop on the tour, giving Beebe the opportunity to explain the habits and life of storks, geese, ducks, hawks, owls, penguins, and exotic birds.

Beebe, at a young age, was not only well on his way to his career as a scientist, but through his work at the zoo and his published articles, he also found himself in the society of New York's rich and famous, the well established in the strata of elite society. This was extremely important in later years as Beebe sought funding for his research and expeditions and sponsorship by the zoological society. In midsummer of 1901, Beebe went on his first expedition sponsored by the zoo. Government funding was not available at that time, and the importance of support by moneyed and interested donors was major. Among the other naturalists and scientists of the day, William Beebe became well respected and sought after. His ability to write about his findings in language of general appeal resulted in heartfelt expressions of appreciation of the natural world which were well received in society of the time. Beebe's fame as a writer was also well established.

Scientific development of the day was becoming more specialized as consideration of the role the environment had to play in the mutation of species grew. In an article Beebe wrote for *Scribner's*, Roosevelt noted Beebe's approach to science:

> *The scientist must be able to see, and to understand what he sees; to interpret what he has seen in the light of wide knowledge; and finally to record it with comprehensive vividness and charm no less than with accurate fidelity to fact, and Mr. William Beebe is one of the scientific men who can study it as it ought to be studied (Remarkable Life 192).*

A friendship developed between the two men with admiration on both sides. It was Roosevelt's awareness of the fragile ecological balance that drew Beebe and Roosevelt together. The developing friendship was setting the stage for circumstances that opened opportunities for Beebe.

In the following year, 1902, Beebe married Mary Blair, whom he referred to as just Blair. She was also a writer who was as eager to travel, explore, and write as was Beebe. Together, they forged ahead with sponsored trips to Venezuela, British Guiana, Mexico, Egypt, Tibet, Borneo, the Himalayas, and Malaysia, which culminated in articles and books written by husband and wife. Their partnership appeared to be a "marriage of the minds." Beebe's concentration at the time was research on the life of pheasants regarding mutations and natural selection. Fame and popular support followed as Beebe was regarded as a distinguished ornithologist and explorer. He was made one of the honorary members of the Explorers Club, to which Roosevelt, Shackleton, Scott, and Lindbergh belonged. At Sagamore Hill, Long Island, New York, where William and Blair Beebe visited Teddy and Edith Roosevelt, discussions of the importance of studies of tropical jungles and ways to explore the depths of the ocean began. Connections made during those happy gatherings, and rubbing of elbows with prominent figures of the time, were Beebe's good fortune and theirs. That he had the funds for his far-flung travels made all the difference.

In 1913, Blair suddenly left Beebe, an act that almost destroyed her heartbroken husband. Articles in the tabloids of Blair's claims against him, although unsubstantiated, brought shame and despondency to a man of private sensibilities. Divorce in 1913 was not looked on with favor. It was a blow Beebe certainly had not seen coming; Blair was the love of his life. With this shattering turn, he dove into his work with further intensity while the friendship with the Roosevelts flourished. Roosevelt's concern for his friend during this time was the reason Roosevelt encouraged Beebe to learn to fly. During World War I, Roosevelt recommended Beebe for a commission teaching student pilots the ABCs of aviation. He was in Europe, then, delaying research, trying to forget Blair, and grateful to Roosevelt for the change.

Again, Roosevelt's encouragement and support, and his influence at the zoological society, resulted in the establishment of a research station for Beebe in the tropical wilderness called Kalacoon, British Guiana. The Roosevelts visited him there as he indulged in research of the interconnection of flora and fauna. Still, the exploration of the ocean depths never left him. There was much to do. He would plunge into his work with even more devotion.

When Roosevelt died at the age of sixty-one in 1919, the last letter he ever wrote was to Beebe, congratulating him and commenting on his work regarding the research of pheasants which Beebe had carried on in far flung places all over the world. Beebe's depression, which returned to him at intervals throughout his life, was now deepened with the loss of his friend. It was almost too much to bear. He once again turned to the salvation of his work and reached for a new frontier, the ocean.

His reputation never wavered. As a scientist who was recognized in scientific circles and who was also known for his personable style of writing and his keen attention to adding to the collections of animals and birds he brought to the Bronx Zoo, all of it easily accessible, he was now, at the age of forty-eight, obsessed with obtaining hundreds, thousands, maybe millions of sea life samples that had never before been seen or recorded, sea life that clung to the seaweed, that spawned and possibly lived within it permanently, and sea life living a mile down, adapted and equipped with what was needed for the extreme pressure of the ocean water and the lack of light.

For years, he'd been dreaming of that world which had not yet been explored. He wrote:

> *The time is not far distant when the bottom of the sea will be the only place where primeval wildness will not have been defiled or destroyed by man. He may sail his ships above, peer downward, even dare to descend a few feet in a suit of rubber or a marine boat, or he may scratch a tiny furrow for a few yards with a dredge, but that is all* (*Remarkable Life* 105).

It is likely that Beebe had a sense of what was to come. Entwined in his thirst for knowledge was also respect for living creatures and the earth itself. As early as 1906 he wrote:

> *The beauty and genius of a work of art may be preconceived, though its first material expression be destroyed; a vanished harmony may yet again inspire the composer, but when the last individual of a race of living beings breathes no more, another heaven and another earth must pass before such a one can be again (Remarkable Life, The Bird, Journal, 1906).*

Beebe was not afraid of danger and was so driven by curiosity that he would forge ahead under any circumstance. On the expedition of the *Arcturus*, in 1925, he was thrilled to descend into the depths of the ocean with the weight of a sixty-pound copper helmet on his shoulders, tethered only by a tube extending from the deck of a small boat where oxygen was piped in from a hand pump. In 1932, he had an iron sphere constructed that enabled him to be the first man to descend a half mile down in the ocean depths, where he viewed the layers of ocean life through a small window. His research not only featured sea life, but the great unknown depths of the ocean that produced creatures coping with the pressure, the darkness, a world so unlike anything mankind had known. And his ability to write about his findings and adventures in a kind of poetic prose that had wide appeal to the general population meant that his work was closely followed.

Now in 1925, with help from several sources for sponsorship, Beebe was ready to make the journey to the Sargasso Sea in the Atlantic and the Galapagos Islands in the Pacific with the newly well-equipped *Arcturus* and a team of scientists of high and varied skills to proceed in studying the ocean depths. It was a dream he almost dared not dream for a long time, but he did anyway. Dreams became intentions became goals became actualities, and the fact that Beebe followed those dreams all the way and back made him famous, particularly given that he was able to record all of it, enriched with his personal perceptions. The public thought very highly of William Beebe. The book that he wrote after the expedition to the Galapagos Islands was *The Arcturus Adventure* (1926) about a journey that was the first of its kind, an exploratory debut study in oceanography taking place mostly in the South Pacific Ocean. It was the beginning of a new view of things taking place in the unexplored and uninviting ocean depths.

Queens, New York, 1958

Sunday afternoon, history unfolds at the white enameled kitchen table in the small Cape Cod on 85th Road in Bellerose, Long Island, New York as William Henry Rohrbein lights another cigarette, pauses, draws in, and goes on in words tinged with what is left of his German accent. He holds the cigarette in his left hand as he is missing fingers on his right. It happened aboard ship, he says, without giving details to the upturned faces before him. Above his palm and on the underside of his forearm is the tattoo of a cross that stands in the path of the orange light of a setting sun and the words "In memory of my Father." The tattoo can't be seen unless he holds out his arm. His daughters used to ask, "Did it hurt?" But it is as if the memory of his father, William Augustus Rohrbein, is so personal it must be kept close to his heart, as if the only tangible evidence he has of having had a father is contained solely in the fact of his death in 1919. He thinks about that night as it still flashes before him in odd moments. He was just eleven years old. It was the war. There was always war.

Ah, well. Laying the cigarette in the solid glass ashtray, he picks up his harmonica, slapping it reed-side down on the leg of his pants, and begins to play *Turkey in the Straw*. It was a favorite on board ship, and brings back a whole gamut of memories, memories his daughters wouldn't believe. What do they know? Their childhoods were easy, secure. They only half listened anyway. They cannot connect with hunger, war, destruction, fear for your life. Thank God. One by one they disappear into the streets to games of softball or roller skating or hopscotch, wandering off to their own secret child lives that he knows nothing about. As for himself, he seems to have missed childhood. He mainly remembers being cold. And there was the darkness that was always accompanied by fear and worry which descended on him from his earliest memories. Left alone with his sister, Lieschen, their cribs side by side, he remembers crying for the missing mother for a long time.

Undaunted, the memories no longer accompanied by so much emotion, he plays on. He steps into another world and gets lost in the sounds as the music fills the kitchen and then some.

He begins playing *Silent Night*, his favorite, but in his head are the ingrained words of *Stille Nacht, heilige Nacht.* He celebrates his home, the fulfillment of what he's always wished for, *Alles Schlaft, einsame wacht.* Now and probably not to stay, this is exactly his feeling. Hard work brought him here, to Queens, out of the city, a step up to be sure, to settle on Long Island with grass and trees aplenty, with neighbors and family. The only connection between it and the past is that the house was built on an abandoned potato field as the city pushed the farms toward the sandy soil of Montauk Point. Here the rich brown earth had pulled him in. It was spelled *established.* Farther out on the island he could still get 100-pound bags of potatoes, which he does faithfully every September and stores them in the bin in the cellar, a sign of his current security that came to him from his years at sea, an assurance of safety from hunger gnawing in his belly in those years between the two world wars. He stayed at sea for ten years. He had work. Not many were as lucky, tales of the depression reaching out to the farthest distances of numerous journeys.

He thinks now of the safety of the house on 85th Road and remembers how, during the early days of the new house, the weeks of rain left a landscape that was a sea of mud, delaying any plans to lay a driveway or a sidewalk. He longed to get to work planting, laying concrete, making his mark in the cement, writing the date of completion. Yet there is, undeniably, a connection with his ancient past somewhere, back when the first four letters of his name *Rohr* had something to do with herbs and *bein* something to do with planting. Yet the past he knows is not of farming but of steel, and he looks on his father's labor, the building of railroad tracks and repairs of trains in the train yard in Bremerhaven, Germany, as everlasting and somewhat above farming. It was the defining skill of his father's hands that made him proud. He has something of his father in him. When he was ten years old, his bedroom in Bremerhaven overlooked the train yard and the miles of smooth intertwining trails of rails from which trains left Bremerhaven on their plaintive journey across war-torn Europe, their lonesome wails filling the night. For him the war had been elsewhere except for the poverty that permeated society, the scarcity of food and money and his father's injuries. Yet the trains also held for him the secret excitement of new places, new land, a kinder home where there was green and sun and warmth and mountains and brooks, places that held the possibility of his leaving. He'd seen pictures in books. Looking back now, the year 1923 was significant. Germany was amid tremendous, catastrophic loss of territory, goods and services and money. They were all caught up in the defeat for a long time.

The apartment on the other side of Bremerhaven, close to Geestemunde where he and his mother and sister lived, had marble stairs and iron railings that spoke of better times. But it was always cold and dark. The winter of 1918 was especially harsh. The rooms were empty of anything but the bare necessities so that there was an echo that reverberated with every slamming of the oak door, which happened when his father appeared. Then the sound of the door was accompanied by a pervading dread, and a substantial bit of fright. He worried about being good. Or good enough.

Now in 1958, his wife and two teenage daughters fill the house with their sounds. However, there is no son. There's no one to carry on the name, *Rohrbein,* and don't forget the umlaut over the *o* that changes the sound from *ror* to *reah.* One should not have to give up an umlaut to be American. He is not good at compromise, keeping that stern look, that demeanor of control in his dark eyes for anyone, particularly his wife and daughters, who might question him or doubt his authority from which the doubt itself springs, doubt that can only be quelled by work. He is an expert at his work, expert at the drawing of plans for the new machinery that will have to accommodate and produce tin cans of any size and shape, where everything depends on the accuracy of the dies and the creation of new machinery—his pay, his house, his family, his security, his identity in this America, and his future in the small Cape Cod in Bellerose, his identity other than a "come over."

No one on the block has a house as well cared for. The lawn is manicured to pure grass, its texture never marred by anything broad-leafed. He waters it every evening in summer, mows it once a week and maybe twice, depending. Bushes are pruned to round domes, hedges cut to sharp corners, shutters frequently taken down and redone. The latter have cut-outs of anchors and that is apropos because he spent a good deal of time at sea before he got married. The shutters are not painted but treated with varnish like woodwork on a ship gleaming with the delight of a well-cared-for deck.

Each morning, he pulls out the grey Dodge, newly acquired after the Second World War ended, and at precisely 6:30 am, heads for the machine shop in Maspeth, in the industrial section at the river's edge, where many fathers disappear into factories. He's escaped city life and the dark narrow streets of the neighboring factories, even though the house on 85th Road is not without worries. There are German immigrant families on the block, along with Irish, Polish, and Italian, but it is the Germans who were closely watched during the war. Of course they were. News of concentration camps in Arizona and Pennsylvania for German immigrants suspected of Nazi ties came through the patchwork of frightened talk. One family had their shortwave radio confiscated by the FBI. Somebody was watching them. So they were, in a sense, less American than the families who were born here. "Come over" as in "When did you come over?"

begins many a conversation, and as a result, William Rohrbein keeps to himself, goes on manicuring his home, and takes enormous pride in it. The other men in the families living on the block sometimes allowed weeds to grow in their driveways. He may be a bit too proud of his heritage, a bit of Aryan perfection left over from Germany's rich cultural history, yet it never occurs to him that that could be a wall between him and his Irish and Italian neighbors. A shyness clings to him. He came from a certain coarseness, a harshness gleaned from a strict and patriarchal society where cleanliness, humility, stubbornness, rules, and hard work were prized, one with its own cruelties connected with anything outside of expected behavior. With it came anger so great it kept everyone in line. Beyond that, there was the second time he had to acknowledge that Germany lost—the First World War, and then the Second, along with the worry that poverty and bombs might again descend here, and for a long time there was always the fright that he might belong nowhere again, or be prosecuted, fitting in only in terms of his skill, his German ability to produce work of great accuracy and attain perfection in the exact measurements that he learned at the age of twelve and thirteen in his last years of school and on the ships until he was twenty-six. Those who work alongside him admire him. He has apprentices and is respected. Here is his heart. Here are the sons, despite his being German and because he is German.

Still, during the war and with the headlights on his car painted half black like sleepy eyes and the buckets of sand in the attic frequently inspected by the air raid warden, and the food rationed and the Victory Garden and the chickens in his backyard, he joined in the war effort with sadness that wouldn't leave.

Not again. Not again. Thank God he wasn't drafted. To fight against his own people was more than any man should be asked to do. And yet, war could come to 85th Road. So sure was he of an invasion by the enemy (his own kind, mind you) or the absolute and fearsome destruction by Hitler of Germany's tradition of knowledge and beauty and regard for music and art and literature and breathless landscape, that all he could do was make a slender, metal disc similar in size to that which appeared top and bottom on every tin can at National Can Company. It was like the dog tags the soldiers wore. It was for his school-aged daughter in case the war came over. On it he engraved her name, *Barbara Rohrbein, Nov. 1, 1937 241-40 85th Road, Bellerose, NY*, and he hung it on a shoelace and made her wear it every day, just in case.

"Ja," he answers gruffly at questions about his past. "I come over in 1924. I vas sixteen only, and not a void of English. Vas on the ships early. The first one vas called the *Arcturus.*"

His daughters took note of how at breakfast he used his knife to scrape his plate clean of any lingering egg yolk. Nothing was to be wasted. He must have known what it was to be hungry, they thought. Always, there was a mystery surrounding their father, with only an occasional peek at the past.

On Sunday afternoons, after chores and the noontime dinner, he sometimes speaks of that past. He plays his harmonica and drifts off into some memories the music brings back, while his foot taps the floor and he pauses to tell about the sea days, the shark they pulled up with a man's watch in its stomach, or the night the birds perched on every wire and there was a lot of poop on deck for him and the other crew members to clean up. He never speaks about the time in Bremerhaven.

But once. He'd walked slowly into the bedroom and pulled out the bottom drawer where his important papers were kept, legal papers—citizenship, completion record from the elementary school in Bellerose where he'd learned English, his union membership, his birth certificate—though it seems impossible that he still has, and pulls from the pile the cardboard-backed photo of his class in Bremerhaven. He was only thirteen then, but it was the end of school for him. He stares at the picture for a long time, unable to remember any names, any friendships, any connections that might have followed him into his new life. He sits in the middle of the class photo of fifty-five boys, all of them with arms folded across their chests, rough, tough, belligerent faces that contain hardness and sadness, not a smile among them, and he wonders how many of them were killed in the second war, how many stayed, how many wore Nazi uniforms, and how many got out in time. In the photograph, directly in front of where he sits are the headmaster and two teachers, arms crossed in example and stern, angry faces as cold as the brick exterior of the school building behind them. He thought of his teachers as men with vengeance in their souls. But maybe not. Maybe that's what it took to discipline a bunch of poor, tough, war-torn, rag-tag and very thin kids. The old Germanic philosophy of beating the little savages into submission. No, he surmises. What he grew up with was respect for authority, fright for his smallish body and an ever-clinging deep humility. But maybe one can have too much of that, he thinks now. Defeat in war stains men's souls. It is a matter of forever trying to uphold worth despite the absence of glory in a far-reaching and lifetime influence.

He stares at himself in the photo, a pale skinny kid in sleeves way too short, his jacket way too tight, his hair brushed smoothly back from his face, an easily made-fun-of boy who has crossed eyes—a boy who wants to learn to play the violin without having one, a boy who shifts for himself from a very young age. Now then. He's come a long way. He hasn't done badly, has he? But at the time of the photo, he had no idea of the portentous years, or the desperation of his mother, or the dangerous, clandestine passage to America, his isolation, or the shape his life was to take, his further education that had nothing to do with school.

His daughters stare at the picture. "That you, Dad? You look smaller than the others. But you're smiling a little. Nobody else is."

He was the scared one. With the smallest share of bravery and aggression.

"*Ja*," he tells them but says no more.

Willi at the Ocean's Edge

And so, the adventure began. Uncle Helmut would always be his hero. His uncle got him a job. He kept that job and many other jobs on the water for ten years. And after he got typhoid, he stayed in the Bronx, and for a short while in Brooklyn, and then in Queens. He had saved money for ten years and has a house that is paid for. He could hear himself saying to his daughters, *I don't vant to hear one single void of complaint from you. About anything. You hear me? You have no idea how lucky you are. And vhen you ask me to teach you how to speak German, I tell you no. You are American. I vant you to be only American.*

Uncle Helmut took him down to the docks in Brooklyn. He was a big wheel with his own shipping company, in charge of a lot of ships and cargo. Willi had never seen ships in Bremerhaven like the one docked at the pier in Brooklyn. It was more like a fancy yacht that might have once belonged to wealthy people. It had been rigged for something unusual as it had an unbelievable number of lines and pulleys that covered the foredeck, and a strange platform resting at the bow, wide enough for a man to stand on, a precarious-looking station from which a man could fish. The man who strode toward Willi now didn't look like a fisherman. He was very tall, wiry and pale, and spoke words that were carefully pronounced. He was not tough like the seamen Willi was used to seeing, raw and cursing, staggering along the streets after the ships came in when they were paid enough to have some beer and schnapps. There was no roughness about Herr Beebe. His eyes were deep set and he was thoughtful-looking like he had other purposes on his mind all the time. He spoke softly and smiled. He put out his hand and said, "*Guten Morgen*!" With just those two words, Willi could tell he was not German, yet the familiar words quieted his fears.

Sitting in his chair in the house on 85th Road now, he thinks it was a miracle really, how he got to be a crew member on a ship of exploration in 1925—how it changed him and made him American. Maybe all his life he's wanted to be back at sea and not be connected to any land at all because it is where all the world's troubles start, where the same conflicts repeat themselves a thousand times. The sea was a new beginning, an introduction to the world between the lands, the world with depths so infinite that it stayed hidden from view until the adventure of the *Arcturus* and the exploration of the South Sea Islands in the Pacific led by William Beebe ending the long, dark silence of that childhood in Bremerhaven.

He knew his explosive impatience with his kids made him fearful to them as he shouted, *You don't know. You just don't know. You have it good, you know. You have no idea.*

The Christmas Gift, 1958

He knew Beebe had written a book, but he'd never seen it. He was not the kind to read books. The *Daily News* was enough. English was not easy to read, and it had taken years for him to speak fluently. He could figure anything out mathematically and he was happiest at working with his hands. It brought him satisfaction and peace. But books? No. Books were too abstract. They told stories that don't matter much, that were pretty much the same. Facts, however, were what a man could depend on.

And now, over thirty-odd years after the fact, the book is in his hands, wrapped in Christmas paper with a red bow, a gift from his oldest daughter with the inscription *Merry Christmas, Dad.* Disappointed, he doesn't know why he is getting a book. Cloth bound in dark green with gold lettering, the book shows wear, yet the pages are still sturdy, rough edged. Before the title page is Plate VIII, Fig. A, the *Argyropelecus*—a luminescent deep-sea fish with eyes directed upward, and Fig. B, a common deep-sea fish with part of the inner fin skeleton visible outside of the body. A note beneath the illustration states that the drawing was twice the natural size of the fish. Twice its size each fit on half a page. This is what he'd missed. This was what the scientists who had gathered around the buckets that contained the haul from the huge deep-sea nets shouted about and exclaimed over. The deep-sea catch. This was what they had scurried off to the laboratory and recorded. He'd always wondered what went on in that lab, what caused all the excitement. And here it is in his hands, thirty-two years later.

The pages are filled with Beebe's scientific text as well as drawings and paintings by illustrators who were aboard the *Arcturus* as it sailed to the South Seas on an exploration of sea life. He knew them all, the scientists, the illustrators, the men who worked the nets, the men who mended them and kept them in order, the men who fed the coal—the stokers, the cooks, the haulers, the party goers, the drinkers, the ones who played an instrument, the ones who walked the boom and drew up the trawlers. But it was William Beebe who led this expedition to the South Sea Islands that he admired most. He was drawn to the man as though Beebe was as accessible as a father but also as distant as royalty. Here was the story, the text written by Beebe himself, the tall, quiet, eager man with a zest for life like no one he'd ever dreamed existed on this earth, the man who described the sea's treasures obtained from depths greater than any that had been found heretofore. Over the years, reminders came about Beebe's work and its importance if you were inclined to read *The New York Times*. Some friends of his supplied him with articles and clippings they came upon which he'd saved in his scrapbook. He still has them.

It was language that was the barrier. And he knew then that he didn't know the half of it, the half that explained everything about the exploration during the sailing of the *Arcturus*.

"How did you get this?" he asks his daughter, his voice suddenly as shaky as his hands.

"A friend found it in a used bookstore in the city," she says. "In The Strand down on Broadway and 12th. I asked her to look for it."

"*Ach du lieber,*" he whispers. "*Gott im Himmel.*"

It is all he can manage.

On the opening page, he reads:

The Arcturus Adventure

by

William Beebe

Director of the Department of Tropical Research

New York Zoological Society

G.P. Putnam's Sons

The Knickerbocker Press

1926

At the time he had no idea about the extensive research that was all around him. He saw the action but not the meaning of it. Still, his heart races now, this many years later, at his unbelievable good luck—to be on that oceanographic expedition of the New York Zoological Society at the age of sixteen. As the ship pulled out of the New York harbor, the Statue of Liberty rose out of the water like a beam of light. Welcome to America. But he was leaving. He was not yet American. Neither would he be a citizen of Germany any longer. He was without a country. He would be floating on the seas between countries, without belonging anywhere. He can see the beauty of it now, how he was pulled away from the aftermath of the First World War and from all the evils man could think up. At the time, he hadn't known that he was going to see a whole other world on that ship—that it was a ship that searched for knowledge and a higher meaning to life. A journey of man's better nature. He feels again that stirring of great hope, that moment when he'd boarded the ship and followed the man too thin to do any real fishing. He understands now how he was drawn to older men, how he'd spent his youth in search of a father, someone to follow, someone's example he could strive toward. Yet in the end, it was his father's example of working with metal that had long ago settled in his bones, and he'd found his way.

Bon Voyage

The *Arcturus* was a twenty-four-hundred-ton steam yacht with five decks and a number of cabins on the top deck. There were American flags flying fore and aft. He thought maybe he would be part of America anyway, since this was an American ship. The *Arcturus.* When he tried to say it out loud, it sounded like *Achtoorus,* like a sneeze. He'd heard the name before. Arcturus was the brightest star in the northern constellation, twenty-five times larger than the sun, the one that sailors used for guidance. That much he knew but little else.

He'd turned to wave goodbye to his uncle, but Helmut Pytlik was nowhere in sight. Instead, he joined the tall man with a mustache who was quite bald. He had difficulty keeping up with Herr Beebe's long strides. Herr Beebe said, "What's your name?" And then again, "*Naameh*?"

"Villiam Henry Rohrbein."

"I am a William, too. William Beebe." And he nodded, still smiling.

"*Ja? Sprechen Sie Deutsch?*"

"*Ich spreche wenig Deutsch.*" (I speak little German.)

He did not know who William Beebe was, but in the coming months, Harry, the cook, wiping his hands on his apron, told him that Herr Beebe was an explorer. Because of him, the *Arcturus* had been bought and outfitted for scientific study.

"The whole world knows about William Beebe," said Harry, waving his hand in the air high above his head, but the boy, Willi, didn't know most of the words in that explanation.

THE DECK WAS STREWN with pulleys, winches, wheels, cables, nets, and lines. A single smokestack rose high above the ship. A boom that could hang way over the side of the boat was pulled upright on deck where there was such confusion he couldn't imagine room for fish, let alone deep-sea fishing. There seemed to be no room for a really big fish. Streamers hung from the top of the two masts to the deck and colorful flags unfurled in the wind. A celebration. A gala?

Herr Beebe took him below decks to the galley. The first thing he noticed was the potato bin, a measure of security for the coming voyage. He knew he would be peeling every potato in it at some time or other, and it would be a pleasure. With a nod, Herr Beebe turned to the steps that led to the upper deck to greet the rest of the crew. Later, Willi found out that in all, there were thirty-eight crew members to be housed below and eighteen expedition members who would be assigned to cabins on the topmost decks. They were not passengers. They were there to work. In the forward cabins there was a laboratory filled with tanks, cages and microscopes, a central workroom with tables laden with drawing and painting equipment, a library of reference books, and a darkroom.

It was February 9, 1925. They would set sail in the morning. Willi wasn't sure where they were going or the purpose of the journey, but he hoped it would be someplace warm. February in New York was as bitterly cold as Bremerhaven. Mid-morning, people began arriving. There were crowds of people who knew each other. Later, Willi found out they were the New York elites, the moneyed privileged. There were women in furs wearing skirts that were shorter than Willi was used to seeing, men in suits, some in fur overcoats and all in fedoras. He knew nothing of them, who they were, what they were about, strangers from a world unbeknownst to him, but they were obviously important, so important that they surely couldn't be interested in fish. Their presence confounded him. William Beebe was in the center of it while the crowd surrounded him. They lingered till midday and then went down the gangplank to gather at the pier. Amidst much waving and shouting from the dock, those aboard prepared to sail. The *Arcturus* left New York harbor at 2:30 on the sunny afternoon of February 10. No one was German. He hadn't heard a familiar word all day.

THEY WOULD BE TRAVELING 13,600 miles in all, stopping at Norfolk, Bermuda, Panama, Cocos Island and the Galapagos. They would be on board for six months. That's what was in the book, but at the time, he hadn't known anything but that the return to New York would be at the end of July. Harry, the ship's cook, said they would cross the Equator eighteen times as he fanned his fingers and counted loudly to teach Willi the numbers, but eighteen made no sense at all. Willi thought it was because of the strange words that he didn't understand, however he read it later in the newspapers. Having to refuel in Panama City was the reason for the repeated crossings.

At the lower end of the bay, a milky white fog descended. Fog on a city or farm still held security with solid ground underfoot, but fog over water lent nothing you could count on. The ship moved forward with only a muffled sound, dark water like silk on either side and beyond, voices muffled and echoed, the wet air clinging to skin and a slippery deck that made it so no one could be sure of anything, particularly direction. They were contained, hugged in by the fog where sound and the edges of everything were swallowed. Then an order came through: they would anchor and wait it out. Sounds stayed close, engulfed in dampness. However, there was time now to achieve some semblance of order. Places were assigned. Willi found his bunk and cleaning implements with which to help clean the decks. He soon found out that "Hey, you!" meant him and that it also meant *mahkh schnell*. Hurry up. Then the chef, Harry, broad-shouldered and with a figure that showed he enjoyed his food, through heavy jowls and a superfluous beard, explained. On a map pinned on the galley wall, his thick finger pointed to Manhattan and then south to Newport News, Virginia, where they would load coal. The meal would suit the gale winds and heavy seas. No soup or anything that could spill. Mashed potatoes for one. There was a baker in the galley, too. His name was Lumpy. Maybe they meant grumpy. He didn't smile much but the smell of baking bread and cakes was the very best part of being in the galley.

Willi watched as Harry pointed at the potatoes. He nodded and began peeling. He would not go hungry. He would even eat them raw like apples.

WHEN THEY PULLED INTO Newport News, more people came on board. They brought luggage and equipment such as cameras and painting supplies. *Hardly fishing equipment,* thought Willi. Then, too, they came loaded with packages and bags of things bought at the five and ten cents store, as though they were worried they would run out of necessities. It was to be a long journey then? Six months, Harry said, using his fingers again to count out the months. This time, Harry made him repeat the numbers again and again until he knew them.

He had plenty of questions but didn't know how to ask them. The weather cleared, but the fog remained within him. He didn't know much of anything other than the sea sickness that was beginning to plague him again. He was not alone. Everyone looked pale. Harry must have noticed the look on his face because he cut off the heel of a loaf of bread and holding the piece in the air said "heel," while Willi said "*kruster.*" Pointing to his pocket, Harry motioned that Willi should keep the *kruster* there and puffing out his cheek and moving his jaw up and down, told Willi to always keep a bite of it in his mouth. Willi noticed not everyone was able to attend dinner. He was not the only one with the constant threat of seasickness, that plague of rough seas, although Beebe himself did not appear to be bothered by it at all and always ate a full meal.

After refueling at Newport News, Harry pointed to the map again. They were headed for Bermuda. “It will be warm,” said Harry, “and the water calmer and very blue. Blue and green actually. You’ll see. Start peelin’ ’em potatoes, eh?” Soon it was not necessary for Harry to point to everything. How quickly the English words came.

Harry was Irish. It was important to know these things. And yet, this being Willi’s first experience with a nationality different from his own, Harry was not what he had expected. Nothing was in the realm of lesser or any of the unfavorable conclusions he’d grown up with. Harry was just Harry. And spoke in a calm manner. The worst thing that could happen was that Willi would wind up speaking English with an Irish accent. The thought made him laugh; the sound of his own laughter startled him as if he’d forgotten how. He bent over the potato, the skin coming off in a brown strip and dropping to the pail below, the knife catching a ray of sun. The knife was dull. He’d watched *Mutter* with the sharpener, the *skrit skrit* of the knife against it, over, under, over, under, the floorboards creaking under her weight, the whole action speaking of strength and intent. He did the same.

When he was off duty in the galley, with preparations for the chicken soup or stew taken care of and meals brought to the dining room and requests for coffee or tea fulfilled, when he wasn’t washing dishes and cleaning up, he was free to roam the ship. The air was warmer on the top deck. He would not be cold, maybe not ever again.

There were twelve smaller boats, like lifeboats. Two of them had glass bottoms. Down below, there were dark-rooms, refrigerators and oceanographic apparatus, and farther below was where they mended the nets that hung from the ceiling in long drapes and where buckets were stored along with flat containers which were not used for cooking.

Yet it was the experience of the sea itself that brought on loneliness. The great advance, the loss of sighting any land, the horizon line with the sun either rising out of it or disappearing into it with an orange sky in the morning or at dusk—it was all the same. At night, just before sleep, he would think of home. Of the train yard, of Germany, and he went to sleep listening for the wail of the trains and click-clack of the iron wheels, steel against steel, and the long low whistle, the pushing on in a solid predetermined path. He wanted to hear them again, the security of those rails spelling out a definite passage, whereas on the restless sea they were all subject to constant motion, merely floating, attuned to the moods of the wind, and blinded by the fog. Nothing was solid and the only known was the motion of the boat. He doubted the men in charge would always know exactly where they were. The Arcturus star wasn't always visible, and the unpredictable waves and gathering winds could change the path of the ship. Mostly it was the wind that decided things, the nebulous, invisible wind. Willi would turn away from the sea to his bunk, knowing that he didn't trust anything. He wanted to go home. He was missing a place where he was unhappy yet the intensity of wanting to belong somewhere consumed him. He'd been pulled out of one culture into another. Germany was lost, disintegrated, fatally wounded. Where were the traces now of high culture, of thinkers, artists, writers, philosophers, scientists and engineers he had learned about in school?

It occurs to him now, in full measure, how great the loss was. At sixteen, he had hoped Germany would not vanish like something dropped into the sea, irretrievable, the last shred of all he had known. He had a vague hope for rebuilding. Maybe he should think about that.

He hid in silence. That's what losers from war do, he figured. There was this puzzling dichotomy of words, this drifting on the unbounded sea against the search for knowledge, for hard facts, beneath. Besides discovery, what would be the connection to mankind? Why this path? What was its meaning? That German mess boy on board didn't know, but now in his fifty-third year, staring out the living room window on a quiet, tree-lined street in Queens—he knows. It all had to be earned. The way was harder for a "come here" than anyone who was born American. Especially for those of German descent. He would have to swallow his pride and his shame.

A WEEK AFTER THEY set sail, the small platform that was called the pulpit was swung over the bow of the ship and lowered almost to water level. It could be raised and lowered as it sometimes dipped into the sea. Most of the time the pulpit hung just above the water and the men descended to it via a rope ladder. They scooped with nets for a long time, but didn't catch anything but seaweed, which they then looked through carefully, finding only a few crabs and shrimp, but no fish. What was it they expected to find, and if no fish, what was planned for dinner?

Mornings, the ship was surrounded by tunnies and flying fish that were as swift as violent torpedoes. They disappeared when the dolphins appeared and what followed was a playful display of easy leaps, a delight to watch. Besides, they always looked as if they were smiling.

Harry said, "You like dolphins? They say they are the souls of drowned sailors." All of which fell on deaf ears. Harry knew that, of course, and repeated the words again and again at different times, but Willi just shrugged his shoulders.

At last, after several days of rough weather, the sea calmed down and the days grew warmer. They sailed into the harbor in Bermuda. *Ve sailed*, he said to himself. He had begun to think of the ship and all its humans as "we." From his spot on the railing along the third deck, which now had become his station whenever he had a free moment, he watched the blue-green water that lay among the marshes in quiet splendor and lifted his head to the warm air. Maybe he had come to a moment that was some sort of heaven, a window in time that let him know the harshness of the life he came from could be erased by scenes such as this, as though he could pull down a shade and hide away all that came before.

Ah, but for this moment in his chair in the living room with the book in hand and a repertoire of memories, he knows one never forgets anything of significance or insignificance, but is always fired with feelings that are carried in brain cells so deep without a man realizing how they leak out in unexpected moments. Anxiety remains, holding scars intact until he acts out in a harshness that surprises even him, never seeing himself clearly. But the view of the blue-green water he is determined to keep in his heart, the place where good things like happiness comes from. He pulls the memory out whenever he needs it.

WHEN THEY DOCKED IN Bermuda, he was glad to see they'd picked up a cat. The rats on board were a problem. The monkey, Chiriqui, that belonged to Herr Beebe, was a kind of mascot as it had been on two previous voyages with Beebe, but Chiriqui was no help with rats. What it did provide was mischief and entertainment, and it didn't mind when Willi spoke to it in German. There was another language that needed no translation, one that music and animals brought about that crossed any barrier. Willi grew attached to both the cat and Chiriqui and brought snacks for them from the kitchen. During the night, Chiriqui slept in Herr Beebe's cabin, sometimes leaping on his chest to wake him, to Beebe's amusement. He heard Herr Beebe talk about it at breakfast, while reaching for his coffee with his long thin arm. Herr Beebe loved telling stories, loved entertaining the staff at breakfast. He enjoyed making everyone laugh. Maybe it was to chase away his sadness. After dinner sometimes, after a drink of beer, Beebe's face seemed to sink into itself. But not for long, as if he remembered his duty as leader, as headmaster, as boss. Maybe it was the responsibility of it all. So much invested and so much faith in him by his sponsors and his responsibility to them.

They entered the Gulf Stream and while the water was choppy, the air was pleasant. Willi was able to take off the too-small jacket he'd come over with and trade it for two cotton shirts that

Harry had given him. He took very good care to keep them clean. They were white, like Harry's. Cleanliness was part of the German heritage, the last vestige of his former home where there'd not been much else. He thought of *Mutter*, not with longing, but with a sense of his grown-up self. He didn't know if he was any taller, but he thought he must be. If she could see him now...

Harry pointed to the map on the wall again. To the east of Bermuda lay the Sargasso Sea. "A sea within a sea," said Harry. Then Harry laughed. "You'll see," he said.

The Sargasso Sea, 1925

In the middle of the Atlantic Ocean, off the east coast of Bermuda, the Sargasso Sea has no land boundaries but is surrounded by currents moving clockwise in an ocean-size circle. Bound by the Gulf Stream on the west, the North Atlantic Current on the north, the Canary Current off the coast of Africa on the east, and the North Equatorial Current on the south, it has been called "the sea within a sea." Here lies a vast network of *sargassum* seaweed that at times appears as a convoluted brown mat. Other times it is green and yellow.

In his research, Beebe read Christopher Columbus's diary and ship logs that revealed hope that they were near land as the vegetation was thick and thought to be drifting off undiscovered shores. Men traveling the ocean with Columbus told stories of the *sargassum* weed being thick enough to cause ships that were in its grasp to sink. However, this had never been proven.

Beebe planned to head for the Sargasso Sea and then on to Panama and the Galapagos Islands by way of the Humboldt Current. The *Arcturus* was well equipped. With a long sea voyage ahead of him that would be filled with observing, trawling and netting, sorting, organizing and illustrating in the laboratories, with chemical research thrown in, it was the fulfillment of a lifelong passion.

The staff he brought with him were all experts in the field of oceanography. W.K. Gregory was Associate in Vertebrates; C.J. Fish, an expert in Crustacea; John Tee-Van, General Assistant (a dear friend in actuality) on whom Beebe relied for general assistance; Isabel Cooper, Helen Tee-Van, and Harry Hoffman, scientific artists; Ruth Rose, an actress turned writer and historian; and M.D. Fish, who was knowledgeable in larval fish. Also of importance was the photographer E.B. Schoedsack and W.D. Cady, a surgeon. There was only one person whose language skills did not include English, Serge Chetrykin, a Russian and a taxidermist.

On previous trips from New York to British Guiana, Beebe had noted clumps of vegetation that extended over areas as large as one or two acres. He thought the weight and stability of the *Arcturus* would surely handle the deep dredging that would bring up specimens from under and in the seaweed. That's what he'd hoped to find and what he was sure existed, but the Atlantic would not cooperate. The ocean heaved and swelled constantly. Chunks of seaweed lay in small islands, but nothing massive like the thick mats of brown seaweed that previous explorers like Columbus said lay quietly waiting to reveal mysteries, a mass of seaweed so great that it choked the movement of the ships.

In 1923, Beebe had made a voyage to the Sargasso and the Galapagos on the *Noma*, a ship not as well equipped as the *Arcturus.* The seemingly inhospitable islands of the Galapagos only whetted his curiosity as the voyage had not been particularly successful. Streamers of the weed were said to be a mile or two long and moved in waves over the sea, rising and falling with the massive swells of the Atlantic Ocean. Because of its wavy appearance, it was difficult to say just how long the strands of seaweed were. Because of the swells, the movement of the ship was often incessantly violent. There appeared to be small islands of seaweed, but nothing as impressive as previously reported.

Then, too, on that first trip to the Galapagos, the *Noma* had been doomed by the lack of fresh water which was difficult to find on the islands, and the heavy use of fuel spent trying to find it made frequent trips back to Panama costly. Also, the terrain of the Galapagos made the islands impenetrable. It was a difficult and non-productive trip. Beebe vowed to try again.

Now, on the trip to the Sargasso in 1925, the *Arcturus* was at the mercy of swells that were the very nature of the Atlantic. Within the huge curving timbers of its interior, the large swells created eerie creaks and groans of the straining planks that could be deafening. It was difficult to take soundings or continue with the gathering of sea life. Often, the ship sank into the troughs of the sea. Only if it went into the swells head on was there a break from the constant rolling.

Working the nets did not go smoothly. When they were pulled in, they were brought over the side of the ship and detached. The contents were emptied into glass dishes and bowls. During first attempts at using the nets, four of them were hauled in safely, but the fifth net and the largest one was the Peterson trawl. It went down five hundred fathoms but came up this time with its mouth bound by a twist in the chain. It was empty of sea life. Still, the contents of the nets when they could get them down, showed masses of snail eggs, active embryos and skeins of fish eggs. Also, evidence of *Pterophryne* and *Leptacephalus* was common. The latter was the larvae stage of eel, which came in two varieties that when mature would head as far north as Lake Ontario, and the other to the headwaters of the Rhine River in Europe. Beebe noted that the larvae of the *Leptacephalus* were transparent although the jaw and eyes were visible. These were exciting finds.

However, the stokers and officers were not impressed. They thought it was insanity to haul in creatures that were less than three inches long. Maybe to them the expanse of the ocean was a bit boring. They would have loved a bit of excitement. Meanwhile, the scientists were working at every desk, sorting specimens using forceps to disentangle fish from sagittate, crustaceans from jelly fish and squid. Samples were studied, painted, described and classified.

Sometimes when Beebe and his crew put over the dredging net, it came up heavy but with a lurch of the ship split with the weight, and all was dumped back into the sea. Again, and again. They waited for calmer weather and when at last it did happen, they put over a rowboat, but enormous swells curtailed that activity, too. At some point, a decision had to be made. Beebe, who hated to give up on anything, decided they would set out to find the Humboldt Current in the Pacific. It held promise of super large collections in the seaweed along its boundaries, seaweed that would contain a world of sea life.

But Beebe wasn't quite done with the Sargasso Sea. Maybe the Sargasso experienced seasons, he thought, and this was its spring, when growth was still young. He remembered from previous trips through the Sargasso that he could see two or three acres *of a golden-yellow undulating meadow.* To experience it in its early stage and on the only calm day for weeks, Beebe dove into the water and later wrote:

> *Most amazingly I am floating in midspace beneath a dense grape arbor with the sun shining through a mat of yellow-green leaves and the unripe fruit glowing like myriads of jade beads. Then the air becomes chokingly oppressive—I gasp—kick out violently with my feet and shoot up through the tangled mass of olive growth. Dripping like Neptune, wreathed like Bacchus, my head breaks water in mid-ocean in a mass of sargassum weed—a thousand miles from land...I shake the water from my eyes, brush aside the dangling strands and, twisting about, behold the huge bulk of the Arcturus silently lifting and settling a few dozen yards away. This is my first fish-eye-view of the Sargasso Sea, on the only day for weeks which is calm enough for a swim. The thought of a grape arbor as seen from below is more than a simile of these hanging gardens, and far from original, for about three centuries ago a Portuguese spoke of them as salgazo or "little grapes"* (*Arcturus* 3).

Will remembers the day Herr Beebe climbed out of the sea and onto the deck with seaweed and those branches with grape-like buds hanging off him. Beebe was laughing, pleased with his time in the water as if he had just come from a bit of paradise. Reading his description of what he had experienced brought the moment to Will as though he had been there himself. The book might be the first and only book he would ever read because it wasn't made up. It was all true. He was there. On every page is a memory pulled from all the things gathered in his head over the years—bringing him pleasure and answering the many questions he'd had for so long. When Beebe climbed out of the sea, Will would have no idea what he had seen until he read those words on the page all these years later. He is grateful for the words, grateful to see how all the work of the expedition was the means to a greater understanding, how besides the fixing of trawling nets and lowering of the boom, its real purpose was the awareness of a life-giving connection with the quiet world of the vast ocean and Beebe's driven curiosity, and his excitement.

While the German genius of centuries gave way to war and poverty, the American genius was in its heyday. The worlds and backgrounds of the illegitimate immigrant boy he was at sixteen and that of William Beebe at forty-eight couldn't have been farther apart. The fact that their paths crossed in 1925 was one of those strange yet significant happenings in the lives of them both, not in terms of togetherness, but rather, in terms of a parallel existence that when crossed, brought to the boy he was an education heretofore unattainable. Reading page after page, he sees for the first time how worlds other than his own worked. He can see how Beebe's writing fills in what he missed as a boy, when what he saw with his own eyes was only half the story.

It makes him think of his own apprenticeship and how important it is to have young apprentices at National Can. So much can be learned about the motivation needed for direction and skill. He looks after his apprentices with pleasure in the teaching, where patience he never had before is prevalent. It is a way of looking into the future, the giving of yourself to that future, much like what a mother must feel in passing on culture to the children in her care. He wonders if his mother ever saw it that way, but at the same time, the losses surrounding her young life must have been dominated by grave uncertainty. Surviving consumed all her efforts as it consumed them all.

As for Beebe, the voyage was a source of material for the book now in Will's lap. *The Arcturus Adventure* was popular literature in the years following the expedition. Over the years, he'd seen other writings by Beebe in the *National Geographic.* He saved every one of them. Everyone knew who William Beebe was.

When Will returned from the sea that summer of 1925, he made a picture album. There was a small collection of black and white photographs that Herr Schoedsack, the ship's photographer, had given him. Will never did find out where Schoedsack was from but that didn't matter. He just had a strange name. Pasting the treasured pictures and newspaper articles from the *New York Times* on the black pages of an album, Will made a label for the front cover in the fine German lettering he'd been taught in school. He'd carefully printed, *The Arcturus Adventure, William H. Rohrbein, Crew Member, 1925.*

First Albatross, First Fish

Part of his job had been to waken the staff as if he were a human alarm clock, which was fine with him except for the fact that he knew he wasn't pronouncing the words correctly. They always came out "Hallf pass sech." (There was an l in "half." He didn't know why.) When he heard one or two of the crew mocking him, he knew that his accent would always identify his origin. Still, he was proud to have the duty.

But for several mornings, he was replaced a bit earlier by the sound of a tin fish horn that was blown by either the captain or an officer on the bridge. The sound signaled the sight of a living creature that Beebe and his crew should be made aware of. Before long, sleepy people rushed out of their cabins to the sight of a large white bird skimming by. It had an enormous wingspan. It was an albatross, usually a welcome sight, but after five successive days, the thrill was gone and the sound of its early morning cry became a bit of a nuisance.

However, it was the remarkable flight of so large a bird that fascinated Willi, because as Harry later told him, an albatross continues the flight for most of its life, gliding over the surface of the sea. It was known to travel distances of three hundred miles without ever touching land. The only time it did seek out one of the islands was when it was time to mate. Its wingspan was the widest you could ever imagine, about twelve feet. The narrow wings were like knives that could slice the wind as it circled and spiraled, dipped and rose over the water. Its flight was smooth and unencumbered as it coasted upwind, too. It seemed to read the invisible wind and the swells of the dark water and was at one with both.

Willi would stand at the railing hanging on tightly to watch the flight of the bird as the wind blew hard and the rough water surged. Riding into the wind, the bird soared, letting the wind carry it up before the swell and skyward. When it needed to descend, it flapped its wings and gathered speed on the downturn using momentum gathered near the rising swell of water, flapping, flapping, and when rising seemed to relax in its effortless soaring on the upswing.

Willi watched until the bird was a dot in the sky. "An albatross," Harry said later. "It's an albatross. Biggest bird ever. Flies over the ocean and never lands."

Never? Would that be his story, too? Maybe it would be okay if it were so. He imagined this could be a good life. On the water forever. He'd keep that *kruster* of bread in his pocket. *Ja.*

AT SEVEN O'CLOCK, BREAKFAST was served. Bacon and eggs this morning. He had to go below just as a school of dolphins encircled the ship. They always gave a show as they leapt in graceful arcs. He would be late reporting to the kitchen. A longing to stay on deck was becoming stronger. He didn't want to miss anything and lingered long enough to hear Herr Beebe shout for the pulpit to be lowered so he could descend to watch the dolphins. Then he was low enough in the pulpit to appear to be among the dolphins. His shouts caused others to come on deck and watch. Two of the men descended the rope ladder to be with him. Lowered below the bow of the ship with an iron grating at the floor and railings for security, the pulpit was close to the action. The waters of the Sargasso were deep blue and clear. The sight from the pulpit was as close to swimming with the dolphins as one could get, although it looked as though a man could easily be swept into the swirling sea.

In the middle of all the shouting, a return to the galley was necessary, but Willi got a glimpse of the dolphins just before he went below. Their skin was sleek, and their actions were smooth as they rose and dove with hardly any disturbance to the water. They almost looked like they were smiling. You could time their appearance by the fact that they surfaced every three minutes.

After breakfast, the trawls were put overboard. Again, Willi disappeared from the galley, and went up to the top deck as one of the overnight nets was pulled in. Harry rarely complained. Clumps of *sargassum* weed were emptied into the waiting buckets and the scientists sorted through them. The batches were small, and the catch was disappointing, which did not elicit any calling out of what they'd found. Willi strained to see what was in the buckets from a few yards away. Most of the seaweed and its small harvest were swiftly taken to the laboratory. Again and again, what had been pulled up in the nets was so miniature the haul had to be observed under microscopes.

The book tells what the bounty was, snails, fish eggs, crabs, and turtle eggs. None of it visible to Willi as he stood on deck watching, but he did hear some of the crew laughing at the minuscule catch, and he was aware of the silence of the others gathered around the buckets which spoke of their disappointment. The book says the wealth of sea life Beebe had hoped to find was not there. From his observations, he'd decided that this time of year was the Sargasso's Spring. He would come back at the end of the voyage, in full summer, and hope for better luck. Taking a bit of *sargassum* to the laboratory, he wrote that there were many hints of spring, for that *golden yellow undulating meadow* was its spring and summer, but now it was fall and winter. The seaweed would propagate as the old stems sank and the new sprouts broke off and floated. Snail eggs and fish eggs were tangled in the fronds of the weed as well as evidence of rootlets and stolons, or branches that grew out from the base of a plant and produced new plants. The attached berry-like structures would float and support the new shoots of seaweed. Who knew the ocean had seasons? No wonder Herr Beebe was often so tired. He'd stayed up many a night until three working in the laboratory to find evidence of a Sargasso Spring.

The book says that Beebe had made an important observation on the haul brought in by the trawls. It was the appearance of a *leptocrephalus,* an easily forgotten name if you weren't a scientist, and a not so easily seen transparent larval form of eels. Turning the pages of the book and understanding it now for the first time, Will sees the photo of the *leptocrephalus*. Observed under a microscope it must have been possible to understand its nature, but he had no idea about it at the time. It looked like nothing was in the bucket. Beebe described the discovery of putting his hand in the bucket and coming up with a twelve-inch piece of *flexible water*. The only part of its anatomy that could be detected was its eyes, so it looked as if the eyes were swimming alone without a body and later, as the fish died, all but the previously invisible stomach and gills could be seen. The book says that under the microscope, the head looked like a dragon with "long sabre like teeth." During the stages of their growth, eels travel thousands of miles, one species toward the shores of Florida to Canada, and the other toward Europe, some winding up swimming in the Rhine. All that is in the book brought the years back, along with new knowledge of what was. All that time gone by. All of it lights up for him now, an illuminated past, brighter than the actual time, brings him back and back and back to the adventurous past.

The photo of the *leptocrephalus* tells little of the narrative. The structure of the larva needs two things to understand it. The microscope and the words. Beebe's words. There's much to see beyond what eyes can detect. That's what he'd missed. The book is everything now. It holds the things he had wondered about and never knew. The external world, the things you could witness, are never enough. A mere window, he thinks now. A teaser.

The nets fascinated him. He watched as they were plunged into the water, each one for a different purpose. There were several types of trawls and nets, some for the surface, some wide for the larger findings. The Peterson trawl was the largest, extending from lines seven miles long. Four cone-shaped nets were attached to the Peterson trawl and were designed for the careful gathering of plankton. Sent from the foredeck of the ship, these trailed behind as they were lowered into the sea. Placing the nets took expertise so the line would not tangle while in descent. Tangles didn't happen often but when they did it took several men hours to clear the line. Some damaged lines could be mended, but not all.

In addition, there were vertical nets from which temperature and water samples were taken along with soundings from the bottom of the ocean. These were heavily weighted. Many a time he'd watched the careful handling of the nets and the pulleys and gears to raise and lower them. He knew about the difficulties, heard the men yelling and cursing, their sweating bodies gleaming in the sun. With Harry's help, the vocabulary slowly came to him. The shouts of the men as they worked the nets and pulleys accompanied by action helped him understand, but now he fully understood that what they were about was collecting, not fishing for food or industry, but to *find out.* The new word was *explore*. A ship, well equipped and costly, was sent out to the oceans simply to find out what was there. And the shouts of those who pulled up an unknown kind of sea life as they poured over the buckets when the nets were emptied, called him from the galley as often as he could escape. The thrill of that never left him. Whatever was caught in the nets was immediately sent to the laboratory because the colors of the creatures changed so quickly in the air. Some fish, used to the pressure of the deep sea, would explode in the atmosphere of lesser pressure. There was even a sculptor on board, Dwight was his name, who produced exact replicas of the fish he was studying and then painted them in the exact colors.

Now, as he turns the pages of *The Arcturus Adventure,* Will sees that the drawings were many and detailed. He'd never seen them before. Most of the sea life was quickly removed, illustrated, carefully categorized, named and sometimes put in aquariums for observation. Nothing was considered too small to bother with, down to the smallest creatures swimming in the loaded buckets. The illustrations in the book are beautiful, detailing monsters from the deep that might only be six inches in length, with bodies you could barely see, and ugly monstrous jaws for their gathering of food. Everything about their physical make-up told the story of how they lived and survived, a testimony to their adaptation in the dark environment and pressure that increased in the lower depths.

What also interests him now in his later years is the planning, engineering, and building of the special equipment for the expedition. It was metalwork beyond anything he'd ever seen. Besides the pulpit, the upright boom on the port side of the deck was often lowered to a position parallel to the deck and extended out from the ship some thirty feet where the water was less disturbed by the ship. In the case of a swell, the boom could swing far up into the air and return, promising a dunking in the salty water. In time, it was discovered that surface nets set out at the end of the boom yielded more than those that trailed the ship itself, because they were working in water that was undisturbed by the wake of the ship. Both the pulpit and the boom had been transferred from the previous ship, the *Noma,* and installed on the *Arcturus.*

The men, having had the experience of the cable being hauled in too quickly and forming loops and coils that snarled the nets, worked to keep the roll of the drum at a slow speed. They'd learned the hard way. On the morning of February 26th, the large drum was put into commission to set out the Peterson trawl, its net having a mouth of three feet by seven feet. Setting it out from the boom was no problem, but when they hauled it back in, what came up to everyone's shouts was a mass of tangled wire. One hundred meters of wire were destroyed and needed to be spliced together.

One time when the nets were pulled up, Willi watched the end of the trawl being pulled open and emptied into a tub of water. From the brown mesh of the net a small black fish appeared.

In the ship's log Beebe wrote, *The first live fish of the expedition was in this haul, a tiny globular chap, energetic but short-lived. He was christened "Zoop," after our German mess-boy's pronunciation of the first course at dinner* (*Arcturus*, Ship's Log, Feb. 26, 1925, 388)

Those at the dinner table when Beebe announced the name of the new fish laughed, and although Willi was embarrassed, he was delighted, too, and he bowed to applause which was enough to comfort him for the rest of the journey. *Ja!* He was feeling part of things now. Setting the table and serving the food, he got to know everyone. He quickly learned the names of the men and women, the menu and the drink choices. The staff and crew greeted him and smiled. Beebe called him Will. Will called him Herr Beebe. The name used by *Mutter*, Villi, disappeared. He would be Will from now on. That's the name Herr Beebe gave him, the man whose name matched his as if he was his son.

A day or two later, when he was on break, he watched as the trawls with the trailing silk nets were being pulled in. Someone called out, "Beaters!" As the steel cable was being hauled out of the sea, they found that to dry the incoming cable the best method was to beat it with sticks to knock off the water before it reached the drum. For some reason, maybe to keep up the rhythm of the beats on the cable, the men would chant along with the whacking in a rhythm that was undoubtedly a work song. Before he knew it, he grabbed a stick and took a place at the cable. It was, as they say, okay. And good, not *gut*. The English word was softer, close to German and easy to remember. One of the men nodded, Charlie, it might have been, smiled at him and said, "Good." It felt like he was one of the crew.

The huge swells of the Atlantic made it difficult for the staff to get work done. The *Arcturus* rolled and wallowed incessantly. His main task when he was not in the galley was to clean up casks and containers that fell and broke, books in the library that tumbled, inks that spilled, specimens recaptured as they slid across the floor, to say nothing of the staff who were tottering and sliding. Sleep was sporadic in the rolling seas and long hours spent in work and cleanup, until a change of plans was announced. Harry pointed to the map again and told him they would sail to the Panama Canal. Maybe they'd return to the Sargasso on the way back to New York. Will didn't want to hear that. He already hated the idea of going back to New York and didn't want to think about it. Then Harry said, as his hand swept across the map, "We are east of Bermuda and halfway between America and Africa."

By God, he was seeing the world. Well, at least the water that touched all shores. He thought he'd probably grown an inch or two just thinking about it.

Images of the Germany he knew still haunted him just before sleep on those motion-filled nights, like ghosts looming from his departed life in Deutschland—the sounds of the ship horns in the harbor at Bremerhaven and the train wails, the chickens squawking and the cows lowing at his grandfather's farm, the crack of his grandfather's belt on his back, the slam and rattle of the old oak door—and the thought of *Mutter* with the blood-stained pillowcase in her valise as she boarded the ship to America. But that night, images were diminished by the worry that accompanied the sounds of the *Arcturus* tossed about in the swells of the Atlantic. The swells were unbelievably high. Sleep didn't come for a long time. He longed for solid ground.

That night, as he lay in his bunk, remembering turned to listening: the power of the water and wind as the *Arcturus* groaned and strained, the sounds drowned out the sounds from the past and he was aware of the rumble of the winches as the nets were pulled in, the typewriters clacking away in the lab as the scientists wrote up the day's catch, the whirring of the sewing machine as the nets were being mended, the creaks and groans of the huge beams that looked like they'd been part of an old galleon, the shuddering of straining planks all warning of the arrival of another huge swell.

But this night, coming from somewhere on deck, barely decipherable, he heard music, too. Someone was listening to the radio. It was Herr Beebe, who later wrote that they were playing "Hands across the Sea." Beebe's words in the book were,

> *It was beyond words miraculous to realize that the whole atmosphere above this mighty ocean, so clear and silent in the moonlight of the Sargasso Sea, was vibrant with untold hosts of melodies streaming past from all over the world* (*Arcturus* 40).

Reading the words so many years later, Will is reminded of that moment, the magic of music moving through the air, how music spoke to everyone, and like those who wrote the music, one could move toward perfection in this life, never achieving it maybe but at least trying. Something so right it couldn't be improved upon. Something to turn to again and again. Something beyond this world and of it, too. He remembers crying at the sounds that night. Suddenly, he missed all he came from, the good and the bad, the wild hope he'd had for the better. This was better, this day on the water, his growing love affair with the sea. Only for a while. He worried about what would happen to him. He had no papers, mind you, but hope was growing despite a nebulous future. Still, he was worried. He had no papers. It was as if he would be tossed about on the sea forever, the future as silent and dark as what was under the skin of the water, swallowing all his dreams, all because the lack of papers. He wished he could tell the kid he was *It'll all come out in the wash*. Something his mother would say.

He escaped the galley whenever he could. Harry was lenient but let Will know when he was being a bit reckless often after he crept into one of his hiding places and couldn't be found. On the deck he watched the shadow of the ship on the mirror of water. The solitude, the loneliness and quiet of the vessel felt like his own, and his thoughts went back, back to Germany and its singleness and losses in the aftermath of war. All the killing and destruction, all the resulting poverty. Despite the kindness of those aboard, he sometimes felt the shame of being on the loser's side, among the enemy despite his age, and realized those around him might not have ever experienced such a loss of pride and dignity. Was to be German evil in American eyes? Was there nothing that could be salvaged from Germany's past? Or counted on? Even now on this island of a ship floating at the mercy of the sea? And what was his place in all of it? What would it be as he got older? With no papers, he would probably have to go back to Germany.

In the morning, they headed for the canal. Within a few days, the water was calm enough to lower the nets again. *Beautiful weather*, wrote Beebe in the ship's log for March 8th.

NOW, YEARS LATER, TURNING the page in the book, Will remembers the pleasure of the music that night and the peace of the quiet sea that came in the morning, the warm air and light breeze as he stood on the deck watching for the albatross, and he is glad for the words from the book that bring it all back. It is beyond memory. It is deep in his heart. These are the details he needs. It is knowledge that broadened all horizons and made him hopeful again. Maybe the word was *okay.* It would all be okay, and he would leave Bremerhaven for good and not look back. He would be set free. But he didn't know that the past would always be with him, appearing in his nightmares where part of him was always hungry and anxious and terrified.

The Lighted Fish

One night, as the sea lay calm, the deep trawling net was put over. Upon examination of the haul from deeper depths than had previously been explored, small fish appeared that were different from anything seen before. Some of the haul was immediately taken to the darkroom and put in tanks. There was a good deal of shouting. Men and women raced to the darkroom where Beebe later wrote that two fish were seen to cast *sparks of glowing light that moved slowly and erratically about*. These were two deep-sea fishes that remarkably made it alive to a place where the pressure on their bodies was sixteen pounds per square inch as opposed to hundreds of pounds on the small bodies in their habitat. The fish existed *long enough to show those little lights which up to this moment had been gliding about the cold blackness of great depths,* wrote Beebe (*Arcturus* 32)

Beebe called out the name of the long black body *astronesthes,* with long tentacle trailing from its chin. It was luminous for the entire length of its body. The other fish, *oneirodes,* was

> *a globular little fish, chiefly mouth; from the top of its head sprouted an appendage, the upper half of which bent at right angles to the base, and from the*

> *end dangled a tiny light, for all the world like an electric bulb. This hung before the fish as it swam along and presumably attracted the small creatures upon which it fed. Approaching to examine the illumination, they would be engulfed by the gaping mouth, so ridiculously disproportionate to the size of the fish behind it (Arcturus* 33*).*

Will understood none of it at the time. Now he understands. The third illuminated fish was the *myctophum,* or lantern fish, Beebe wrote about. They were spotted all over with little points of light. So that's what all the shouting had been about that night. When the discovery was made, Will had been lying in his bunk after a long day. He would have loved to have seen the cause of the shouting. Now, many years later, he turns to the illustrations in the book, carefully drawn by Isabel Cooper, who was said to have made two hundred paintings and drawings of the fish, and Will realizes his day hadn't been as long as the scientists who were up all night recording, illustrating, sorting and organizing the brilliant haul of the day's catch. He has such respect now not only for the exploration, but the sharing of knowledge that Beebe had seen to and all those who had contributed.

Among the illustrations in the book is the *astronesthes,* or Eater of Stars, that captures his attention now. There is a drawing of the *astronesthes* in pursuit of two lantern fish, which are outlined with a stream of lights along the lower part of their bodies, with scattered lights along the sides. In the drawing done in daylight, the fish chasing the lantern fish was the *astronesthes*, with a tentacle extending from its mouth, a slender tail and six rather large fins. The fish in darkness revealed the luminescence of those fins and tail and tentacle as well as dots of light from its large mouth to its tail. This is the Eater of Stars. *The luminescence of both types of fish is remarkable*, Beebe wrote.

The lantern fish, of an iridescent copper color above and silvery white below, were not more than two inches in length, weighed in at a gram (it would take 450 to make a pound) and getting enough food from plankton to *live, to fight, to migrate up and down, to keep illumined 100 lights and to lay upwards of 1700 eggs.*

Beebe says,

> *Not until I dissected one of the astronesthes did I realize the full significance of its title as Eater of Stars for in each astronesthes I found a full-sized, just swallowed lantern fish. In the dark, this voracious black fellow was a gorgeous sight, the skin covered with a host of minute luminous specks, while the fins fairly glowed with pale green light. Curiously enough, it was the stem, not the specialized tip of the chin tentacle, which was luminescent* (*Arcturus* 218).

A lone sentence stands out: *I hope to approach much closer to the meaning of their lives* (*Arcturus* 219).

Teddy Roosevelt would have approved.

One afternoon, Herr Beebe thought the water had smoothed out enough that they could all go for a swim. Will heard Herr Beebe say at dinner that he hoped that swimming would be part of daily exercise since they would be coming into calmer seas when they reached the Pacific. However, smooth swells deceived them. There was no telling how high they were, despite the pitch of the ship. Beebe dove in first and enjoying those swells and the buoyancy of the salt water, just floated without trying to swim.

> *The swells were smooth but mountain high, not wave-like but as if the whole horizon were a range of mountains marching majestically toward me. I seemed for a long time to be floating on the bottom of a gigantic ultramarine cone, then slowly and gently to rise—high, high, higher—until I dominated the Arcturus and seemed to approach the drifting clouds overhead....I dived and entered an ultramarine world...and sank as low as my stored-up breath permitted, and then before I turned and kicked upward, took one long look beneath, and tried to imagine that unimaginable world of life down, down in the ever blackening, ever greater pressured depths. No ship or companion was visible and my sense of devastating isolation, of cosmic awe can nev-*

> *er again occur with equal force in this life....* (*Arcturus* 35-36).

Some men dove overboard from the deck and the not-so-brave others descended the rope ladder into the water. Will waited on deck, wrapped in fear. He'd never learned how to swim. From the ship, the swells had not looked so high, as the water had smoothed out some. He could see the ship no longer was plowing into the swells but was languishing sideways. Without pushing into the swells, cutting them and riding high and low with the bow slicing the water, the ship lay sideways to the swells and tossed from side to side, wobbling dangerously.

Foolishly, as though he'd dared to prove something, he went down the rope ladder anyway. He shouldn't have. He hung on to the rope in terror. But climbing aboard again was a matter of losing face, to say nothing of losing his life. One minute he was plunged back into the water and the next, slamming high against the side of the ship. Looking at the water from the deck was one thing. To hang onto the deck railing in rough weather was thrilling as one trusted the power of the engines and the movement into the wind. But to feel the power of water against his body—a body that seemed to have no strength of its own—his helplessness was the most terrifying experience he'd ever had. Twice he let go of the rope as he was slammed down into the water again and again. He was going to drown. The men were shouting but he understood nothing. A word escaped from his lips that he would rather have died than say out loud. *Mutter!* The power of water to envelope him and take his breath away! In panic, arms flailing, he shouted out for his *Mutter*. Why in God's name did he do that? He was nothing. He was what they call a wimp. The humiliation of it. Arms lifted him.

"Easy now." It was not the words. It was the tone. Someone lifted him and grabbed him around the waist and pushed him toward the rope ladder. It was Leon, the stoker. He spoke differently from the others. "*Danke*," Will remembered screaming into the wind as he hung onto the rope ladder for dear life despite being slammed into the side of the ship again and again, hoping beyond hope that no one heard him screaming for his mother. Leon was Scandinavian. He had saved Will's life. Will began to wonder then where everyone on board was from. He was beginning to see it mattered and didn't matter, too, that several of the crew were strangers, and not all were American, that no one was German. There was a basic humanity that went beyond language. And now, after so long, Will Rohrbein sees other things—his long voyage from boy to man.

Oh, Mutter. Your son must swim away from the rope, make the break alone—a journey all men must take. Still, I have to cling to the rope ladder for now. There is too much need, too many unanswered questions, a necessity not yet realized. Later. Later I will know the meaning of endings and beginnings, the loss accessed through the window where lies the untamed return of hope. It is a strange exchange and difficult to decipher clearly. But this is clear: Not all the world is as I had once believed. And I am not as I once was.

When Beebe and the rest of them were back on board, the alarm sounded because two whales had been sighted, looking as though they had just been frolicking nearby. Soon after, a dolphin-fish hung onto a trailing hook, which encouraged two of the men to get the fish aboard. When the fish flung itself off the gaff and landed on deck, one of the men locked both arms around the fish and fell with the fish on top of him. Beebe said what was memorable to him was the thought that the fish might have been a direct descendant of the fish Columbus had described in his writings. The *Arcturus* was on the course Columbus had taken, as Beebe's research had revealed. But while Herr Beebe was thinking about the fish and Columbus, a first officer passed by and said, "Well, thank God, somebody's caught a *visible* fish." The word *visible* was new, but Will figured it out. He laughed as he thought so, too, but kept his thoughts to himself, still hoping no one had heard what he had shouted into the wind earlier.

Willi as a young boy (date unknown).

Lieschen and Willi (date unknown).

The Arcturus; from Willi's scrapbook.

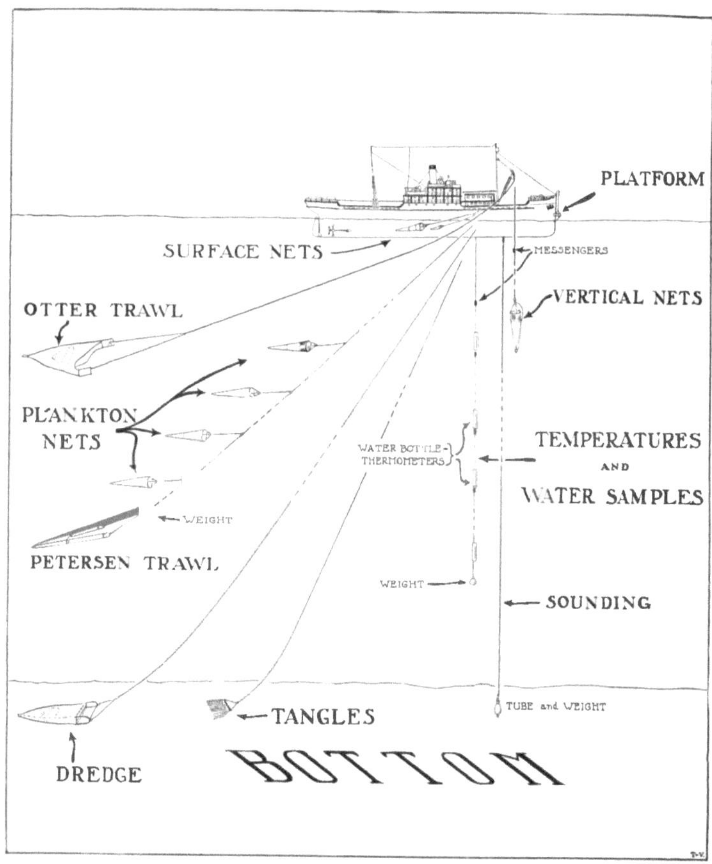

The Arcturus was rigged to trawl and dredge specimens at depths of up to one mile.

A boom-walk allowed the crew to work up to thirty feet away from the side of the ship.

All hands on deck as the day's catch was raised to the surface.

Beebe donned a 60-pound copper helmet with lead weights for his underwater explorations.

A massive manta ray was one of the more memorable catches.

Photographed prior to its capture, the manta measured eighteen feet from side to side.

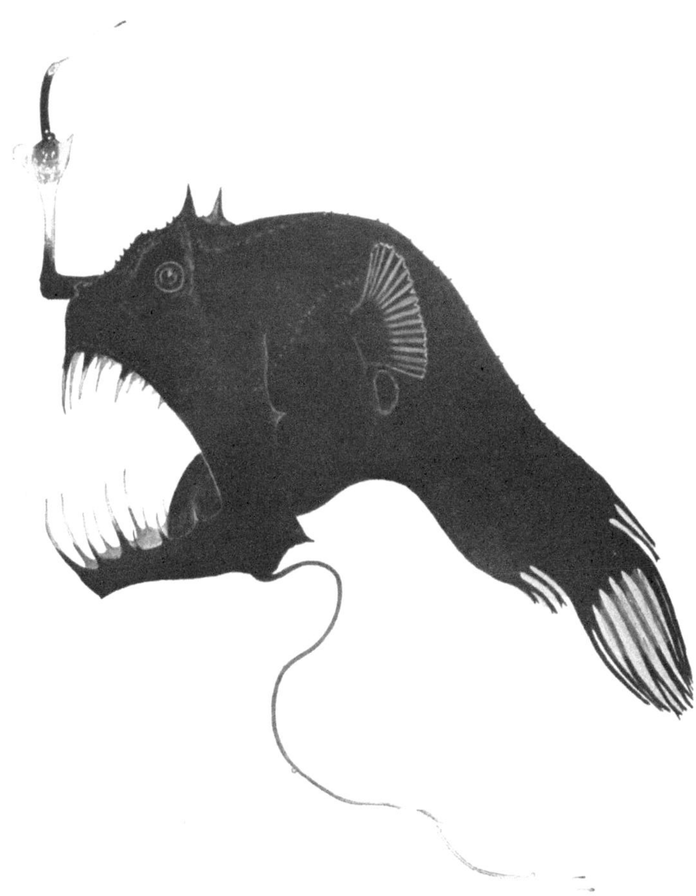

The "little devil" of the Arcturus, Diabolidium arcturi Beebe, shown at three times natural size.

A blind deep-sea fish, Bathypterois sp.

A crowd assembles to welcome the Arcturus home to New York, as it trails a 180-foot celebratory pennant.

William Beebe and John Tee-Van pose next to bathysphere after record-setting dives off Bermuda (Getty Images).

William Beebe (left) and Otis Barton (right) pose next to bathysphere after a dive in this 1931 photo supplied by Beebe to National Geographic.

Clear Passage

They retreated from the Atlantic, heading south while the Atlantic said goodbye in its own ferocious style. The sea was rough, causing the ship to roll the night of March 6th. They were busy in the kitchen cleaning up broken dishes, pots, and utensils that were spread all over the floor. Very little stayed in place. But Herr Beebe sent down the Peterson trawls anyway, two of them, to depths of 500 and 250 fathoms. The haul was the best in several weeks, but that was the end of trawling for a while as the deep swells caused a change in course so that the *Arcturus* could plow into the swells instead of riding them. Then the shaft of the circulation pump broke and that made the engines stop. It was impossible to sleep or stay in the bunks and no one wanted any breakfast. The ship rolled and rolled. The captain decided to head north and try to escape the disorientation and allow those on board to eat lunch and dinner.

It took a few days to get the *Arcturus* functioning properly again and work continued as they headed for the canal. Now the surface of the water was something that could be depended on and they went through the canal with no trouble on March 28.

As they steamed into the Panama Canal, Harry said, "Go watch," pointed to the wall clock and held up ten fingers. "Ten minutes and you be back and help with lunch." He grinned, proud of himself for the strange new word, *Essen,* which he said now as he pointed to the bread laid out for sandwiches, an invitation for Will to help himself.

"Changing your name to Will? Okay. Forget Willi. You're a crew member now. You teach me a little Deutsch and I teach you English. Deal, mon? Off wi' ya noo."

The ship pulled into the lock just as he hurried to the bow. Then everyone was running aft to see the monstrous gates close behind them as water from Gatun Lake drained into the lock. The ship rose to the same level as the water in the next lock. When the gates from the lock in front of them opened, the ship was pulled by cog wheel train into the next lock. He couldn't see all of it but kept running from the galley whenever he could be spared. There were two men (that's all he could see), one of whom conducted from the engine house where he assumed the lever for the locks was controlled. The other one manned the trains on both sides of the canal. There was another man, too, a pilot, who came aboard to guide the ship. He was specially trained and took over for the captain to keep the ship in the channel. The effort, the planning, the time and hard work were a monument to mankind. And all the failures, too. The lives lost. And then the great insistent effort forward.

"It was Roosevelt," said Harry. "He made it happen." The iron gates that swung open and closed were huge, thick masses of steel that didn't close in a straight vertical, but more like that of the peak of a house roof, allowing the gates to withstand the pressure of the water. As the lock filled, the ship was lifted to a higher level each time it entered, and later, lowered in the same way. There were three locks on the Atlantic side of the canal and two on the Pacific side.

By evening, they were on *der Stiller Ozean,* the great Pacific. It was some kind of miracle. As many times as he was to sail the canal, it never got old.

"*Der Stiller Ozean. Verstehe*, Will?" said Herr Beebe at breakfast the next morning over a celebratory breakfast of fried fish and eggs.

"*Ja.*" The German words were music to his ears. But it was the attention he so appreciated. Beebe always looked him in the eye when he spoke to him. His eyes were deep set and he looked at Will with an intensity that seemed like he was doing research even on people. He always took a second to acknowledge Will as he served the meal, and he always said thank you when Will put a plate of food before him. Each time, Will wondered if Beebe knew he was illegal, and if he did know, would he look at him with the same eyes?

Back in the galley, as Harry pulled steaks out of the ice box, he said, "Pickin' up more folk today." Will remembered that steak these many years later. He had never had steak. He couldn't take his eyes off them.

"We in Panama City now. Do a few more potatoes, okay?" Harry held out three fingers. The potatoes reminded Will of the smell of the earth he so missed. Earth dust from solid ground still clung to them and he rubbed his hands against it. Imagine the generosity of steak on board ship with all that fish in the ocean. And fried onions, too. A show of abundance.

There was no time to wonder why, but when they pulled into Panama City, there was a boy waiting on the pier with a woman—probably his mother. Harry said the boy's name was David Putnam. He was twelve years old and he was going to bunk with Dr. Gregory from the Museum of Natural History in one of the forward cabins. So. It was obvious that David not only had a prominent place on board the *Arcturus*, but in the world, too. Harry said David's mother, Dorothy, and his father, George, were friends of Beebe's. As a matter of fact, George Putnam was Beebe's publisher. "You know. He makes books, and Uncle Will writes those books," said David.

"Maybe David and you can be friends," Harry said later.

Ah, no. No. Will looked down at his feet. He knew his place. When they'd docked in Panama City, food was brought aboard that Will had never heard of. David knew all of it. He would come to the galley and ask for a mango, and he knew how to eat it while Will watched. Bananas, too, fried no less. David was from a different world. The divide was too great, and any mingling would be politely discouraged. Maybe not, though. Maybe out on the ocean away from land and all its trimmings and social bias and rules, stated or unstated, all of that wouldn't matter. The kid was always smiling and seemed friendly. He was connected to everyone on board the ship. From the first moment, he called Herr Beebe "Uncle Will," and just like his Uncle Will, he wrote everything down. He carried a pad with him as though he was a reporter. Later, he told Will he was keeping a diary and that it would become a book and it would be published by his father, George Putnam. "You probably never heard of him, but he's famous." To which Will just nodded, not sure of what the kid said, but Harry told him more later.

He was alone, apart, and illegal to boot. Yet grateful. He'd lived with humility all his brief life. He could hide there. Head down. Silent. Like a burglar in the night, stealing glimpses of business on board and yearning to know. Anything. But the foreigner. *Ja.* One with a whole lot of luck to be on this ship, knowing everybody, all of them important people. But the fear inside him remained. Rock solid, it stayed even as the wonders on board ship kept unfolding.

David was a privileged kid. Like he owned everything. The published book would be entitled *David Goes Voyaging* by David Binney Putnam. Since the world was already his, he could smile easily. He was secure and could live with assumptions, to say nothing of a healthy dose of confidence. He would have his thirteenth birthday party aboard the *Arcturus*. Everyone would dress as a pirate. And a song would be written for him. And his birthday present would be a real cutlass from Don Dickerman, that good friend of Herr Beebe, to complete his costume. And when his parents divorced, his new stepmother would be Amelia Earhart.

Ja. You believe it?

It was in *The Daily News* when Amelia Earhart disappeared in 1937. Will was back in the States by then, married and living in Queens when the news broke. *Don't that just beat all. Lost at sea yet. Damn shame. Bad luck comes to everyone equally*, the guys at work said. Will said nothing. The attempt to circle the earth thwarted, the bravery to even try, that beautiful woman with the short locks of hair tossing in the wind, smiling from the cockpit of the airplane—David's stepmother, the epitome of huge hope and daring, lost at sea, and the huge cost of the oceanic search for clues, the haunting sorrow for her and her family. He thought of David then and his notebook and how the future held tragedy no matter what the station in life. How strange that he had crossed paths with David—or with any of them aboard the *Arcturus*. Something out of another era. How much he now misses that time when the very wind held magic and adventure. He is standing on the deck again with the scent of ocean on his skin as he listens to the cries of the birds--his bit of romance even though he was but a mess boy. Illegal to boot. And there was David, with the same diligence as Beebe, recording everything, even a few sentences about Will without malice or judgement.

He knew little about how the rest of the world worked back then, but he had had a glimpse of another brighter, easier time that most of the people on board had enjoyed. Stories told during mealtimes and the ensuing laughter proved it. Thinking about it now as he sits reading the book, there was something about that voyage that reflected the times, the Jazz Age—the daring and hope, the money to carry out an expedition such as this, the knowledge that war was elsewhere, yet the endeavor and seriousness of the work, celebrated with music and laughter with a blindness as to what would come, and then later, the Depression, when the bottom fell out.

But when that happened, he was lucky. He was okay. Ever so grateful to have a job, he remained on the ships during the worst of times. It was steady work. But that year on the *Arcturus,* the very air was filled with enormous possibilities, dreams of flight and exploration, and with money to do so, adventures sprang up everywhere. Inherent in the preparation for the journey was the dichotomy of responsibility and freedom, each requiring a serious consciousness.

From the first day, Harry couldn't stop talking about David and the Putnams and Beebe. Harry told him that Dr. Beebe (he always called him "Doctor") had invited David and his mother, Dorothy Putnam, to come with them on the *Arcturus* journey in appreciation for the support and funding for Beebe's expeditions. George Putnam and his wife, Dorothy, were close friends of Amelia Earhart. For David, it meant he had had permission to leave school for the trip. He would have a tutor on his return to New York.

A while later, when Will was in the States for a few weeks, he found an article in the *Daily News* about the Putnam family and learned that Dorothy Putnam and David's tutor had had an affair. The tutor was quite a bit younger than Dorothy. *Scandalous,* said the *Daily News*. It meant that George and Dorothy Putnam would divorce, and in the upswing of things, Amelia Earhart, Dorothy's good friend, would become George Putnam's new wife and David's stepmother. For this stowaway immigrant, a bit of pride, then, because he knew them. He knew how they liked their coffee.

His Tante Anna would say, her lips tucked in at the corners, "Humph, high muck a mucks. Don't think you're special because you know them." He would answer that Beebe was a hardworking man devoted to his goal. He wore shorts, old faded shirts and sometimes a pith helmet. His collar hung open and his hands were always in the salty brine skimming through the plethora of tiny fish and whatnot with his captivating and inspirational seriousness, the sweat pouring off his brow, his fingers wrinkled as he pulled minute and strange life out of water. Beebe did real dedicated work. It occurs to Will now that he never saw Beebe angry. He was quiet and absorbed. He never seemed to have time for anger or impatience.

With the book in his lap, thirty years after the fact, Will realizes there must have been long absences and very busy careers for David's parents. In that way, David and he had something in common. Families had broken apart for them both, for better or worse, by intention or fate. David was already on a path where the silver spoon promised fame and fortune and on top of all that, he would have a book published at the age of twelve with a forward by William Beebe. Imagine that. Will wondered if David ever mentioned him in his *David Goes Voyaging*. As a matter of fact, he did, as Will found out later.

> *Soon after dawn each day one of the crew washes the decks. And it seems only a short time later that Willie, the German mess boy calls Hallf pass seex* (*David Goes Voyaging* 73).

No. What he was saying was *sechs. Hallf pass sechs.* He still says it that way. And he still doesn't know why *half* has an *l* though he has dutifully pronounced it all his life. His daughters enjoy correcting him but he likes the sound of the l and f together, like a loose thread of German.

Here was the window into the future. For him, life would carry hard work and responsibility with absolutely no favors from anyone. David represented another life, one of position and riches and comfort in an America where it was true when they said anything was possible, even though that was mostly meant for those of a certain station. In his youth, Will could never have imagined such a life, but he looks at it now with respect, if not awe, although evidence of social status angered him at first. He acknowledges to himself that he was jealous, but that was kid stuff. Probably in that top social station, the rules were broken for them or by them. Old money backed them up.

It was none of his business. As naive as he was, he believed German men didn't leave their wives. Divorce was a thing of shame and forbidden by the church. There were rules that were not to be broken. It's just the way it was. David and his family were established Americans. With a name like Rohrbein and his accent, Will would always be marked. There is no real melting pot as far as he can see. People of like backgrounds hung together. He wondered if he would ever be accepted elsewhere, but as the years went by, it no longer mattered as much, as he came to realize that what binds men is the camaraderie of work. His friends now are Sotie from Greece, Albert from Austria, and Franz from Poland. None of it matters, yet to identify that origin is important to each of them. These are men he knew during his ten years at sea. They all wound up at National Can Corporation where each of them has had long careers, job stability, and good pay, thanks to the Machinist Union. At sixteen he was still wet behind the ears, his mother would have said. Through the years, he became part of America and it was because of his skill, his work.

Now, as he turns to the next page *of The Arcturus Adventure*, he wonders whatever happened to David Putnam. He knew David went on other expeditions, because two years after the Arcturus, in 1927, there was a cartoon in *The New York Times.* The headline read, *Envy of United States Boyhood, 14-Year-Old David, Goes Adventuring Again*. Above the series of illustrations were the following captions:

> The hero of his own novel, "David Goes Avoyaging," young David Binney Putnam, son of the publisher, was only 12 when he went on the Beebe expedition into southern seas. Adventure has again lured the boy, and he is now sailing toward Greenland on the schooner Morrissey. Soon he will be at home among the icebergs and the polar bears. A romance for which any healthy boy would give the world, will lie at his doorstep. He will see gigantic icebergs sail majestically by. He will hunt the biggest of big game. The life of a boy of the Eskimos will be his for a few months. He will learn to trail, to stalk, to trap and kill from the experts of the North. Do you envy him, boys? (*The New York Times*, 1927)

Ah yes. There it was, that last a bit much, pointing out the difference between the classes, and the great distance between privileged opportunity and the striving of the poor, plain as day. Will acknowledged there was no fighting it. Besides, for him there was comfort in work. Turns out, that is what it was for Beebe, too. He'd read about periods of depression that Beebe had, and his wife leaving him. Depression for Beebe spelled weakness for which the only solution was greater focus on work. As for Will, he had been on the Arcturus, right there with David as he took notes, eating the same food, knowing who William Beebe was and seeing how devoted he was to his work. But did David know his good fortune? Will didn't think so. One had to compare situations, be aware of the lives of others and the scars of history to come to that place where real knowledge lies, an education that didn't come through books.

In time, the potato bin had fewer potatoes. He had peeled a good number of them by now. He measured his time by the number still in the bin, dreading the foreseeable empty potato bin measuring the end of this adventure. When he got back to New York that summer of 1925, he cut out the saved cartoon about David and pasted it in his album. This was *his* book and he kept it all his life to pass on to his kids, who would find it in the same drawer as the picture from school, those fifty-five young and unsmiling boys, who probably never made it out of Germany in time. Just before Hitler when the world turned upside down. As one of German descent, he felt he was tainted for life. But no. It didn't happen. All else falls away when you realize that the only thing that matters is your ability to do your job. Sometimes he wonders though, what else there might have been.

Now, looking back, he knows one thing. Despite all, the love of Germany never left him. The mother tongue and the music, the beauty of the countryside, the history of composers and poets and artists. Since he'd left in his youth, Germanic youth was his youth, his identity, and there would always be hope Germany would return to greatness. Germany was part of his own promise. Especially after the Second World War, especially with the Marshall Plan when there was so much momentum for good. But who can remember with any amount of accuracy what one felt at sixteen except for the homesickness which returned night after night until slowly what was taking place around him on the *Arcturus* drew him in. And memory now centers on all that had happened and his connection to it. And he knows, all told, the months on the *Arcturus* were the best of his life. But lingering still, in the middle of all of it, there is an abiding love for his native country. It is in his blood and it runs deep. Would there always be that wall? Would he ever grow beyond it? He could see that it was his responsibility to scale that wall. He could see now the probable of the fate of those who never could. But America still has opportunities to offer. He believes it.

When he gets lost in his own thoughts, the book pulls him back. Beebe speaks of walls in an entirely different way, of course. What did he know of not belonging? Beebe was concerned with the intriguing scope of wildlife, wild plants and trees that seemed to collect and grow along walls on solid ground. It was a view that went way beyond individual histories. Along walls of stone and wooden fences appear those things not wanted elsewhere in cultivated land. A kind of excess, maybe, a happening with its own richness. A pooling of resources overlooked or unwanted, gathered anyway, like migrants searching possibility. There was, finally, the interconnectedness of all life.

In 1923, in his book, *Jungle Days*, Beebe included a poem, *A Chain of Life:*

This is the story of Opalina
Who lived in the Tad,
Who became the Frog,
Who was eaten by Fish
Who nourished the Snake
Who was caught by the Owl,
But fed the Vulture,
Who was shot by Me,
Who wrote this Tale,
Which the Editor took,
And Published it Here,
To be read by You,
The last in The Chain,
Of Life in the tropical Jungle.

Is this the story of humans—to be lost in the chain of chaos that men cause, defeating the other, rising to power? They were a singular entity, alone with no predator to conquer them, they became the conqueror, the last vestige in the chain, eternally hungry.

The Stiller Ocean

Beebe's previous expedition aboard the *Noma* and the significance of the Humboldt Current was his introduction to walls that existed in water as well as on land. Beebe was looking forward to going in a northwesterly direction toward the Humboldt Current, the very opposite of the Gulf Stream which it met mid-ocean, a strange paradox that not only held a promising exploration of fish and birds, but a further investigation of the presence of penguins so close to the Equator. Swimming in these waters meant enjoying the pleasure of a warm, summery current only to suddenly come up against a shocking wall of freezing temperatures. On his previous journey to the Humboldt Current two years before, he was startled by the drop in temperature that might require sweaters as they crossed the Equator.

He'd studied the work of men before him such as Sir John Murray and Johan Hjort who, sailing on the *Michael Sars* in 1910, took careful readings of temperatures and depths and photographic recordings including drawings of deep-sea fish and microscopic animals. Being limited by the equipment of the time, theirs was only a random sampling of life in the depths. Now, in a ship that boasted increased speed and powerful winches, Beebe hoped to do much more. It was the ability to achieve investigation of greater depths that intrigued Beebe. In the lab, they kept careful readings of the contour of the ocean floor.

THE VOYAGE OF THE *Arcturus* in 1925 followed by two years Beebe's initial expedition to the Galapagos Islands on the steam yacht *Noma*. Inspired by Charles Darwin's observations of finches and giant tortoises on the Galapagos, Beebe sought further evidence for the great Victorian's theory of evolution. It was a year in which controversy boiled. The epic clash of Clarence Darrow and William Jennings Bryan in the Tennessee Scopes trial drew worldwide attention. Always a hard worker, Beebe was energized.

Despite problems on the *Noma*, Beebe wrote and published an account of the expedition called *Galapagos: World's End* upon returning to New York in 1923. The publisher was George Putnam, close friend and supporter—and young David's father. The book was extremely popular and within three weeks, a new batch of books had to be printed, a situation envied by any writer and testimony to the public's regard of Beebe. Returning to the Galapagos for further exploration was always on his mind. The plan was to investigate the Sargasso Sea on the way south.

TWO YEARS LATER, ON the *Arcturus* in 1925, Beebe noted that the Sargasso Sea of the Atlantic could be described at that time as a desert. Now that they were in the Pacific, what he found were the gentle ripples of summer seas and a fertile valley rich in sea life. The crew reveled in the smoothness of the water and the pleasant calm of Der Stiller Ocean. On the third day of sailing, Beebe knew they should be near the Humboldt Current, but he awoke one morning to a message from the captain that a rip tide could be seen in the distance, a line of foam harboring many species of birds flying above and resting on floating logs *picking out edibles from the crevices.*

Beebe wrote: *here was a concentration of organisms greater than I have ever seen—so abundant that in places they were of the consistency of soup* (*Arcturus* 45). Nets put overboard earlier had to be withdrawn as they quickly grew heavy with sea life and were in danger of breaking. The nets also were often swept under the keel of the *Arcturus* and close to the engine propellers. Fifteen minutes of towing was all the nets could take, even the ones made of rope and some of the finest silk. For much of the time, the forward deck was filled with all kinds of paraphernalia.

However, there simply was no evidence of Humboldt Current. The rip tide they were now experiencing must have been a recent development created by the absence of the Humboldt, which somehow had been deflected. The Humboldt seemed to be as elusive as the Sargasso Sea. Instead, there was this rip tide, a definite line, a wall in the ocean, a place where two currents of ocean water did not mix but showed an unlikely but defining boundary, clearly marked by the line of froth. Contrasted with previous observations in writings about the Humboldt Current, the temperature on both sides of the line showed only a few degrees difference.

The line itself was composed of logs and all sorts of flotsam and jetsam where two warm westerly flowing streams of water, two hundred miles off Cocos Island, stretched from horizon to horizon. It had floated and collected here, providing a home, a nursery, and an eatery to which clung a concentration of organisms more opulent than Beebe had ever seen. Above, birds gathered. Boobies, petrels, sandpipers, and frigates filled the sky and landed on the logs, feeding on life the logs sustained.

To the south, the water was dark and rougher than on the northern side of the "wall" where the water was of lighter color and smoother. Foam marked the coming together of the two currents and formed a zigzagging line with white caps breaking through the froth. Sandpipers that were known to nest in Alaska followed the foam and the *Arcturus* was soon surrounded by five or six hundred dolphins. The nets proved to be quickly filled with floating organisms and were strained with the abundance of sea life. Now the pulpit came into regular use. Often in the Atlantic, those standing on the pulpit found themselves swept under the waves, but with the use of hand lines and dip nets from the pulpit, the gathering of specimens now proved easier. Access was also greater when both the gangway and the boom walk were lowered. The scientists and crew caught fish of all sizes, from five-inch triggers to sharks.

The real challenge was to bring aboard one of the logs that gathered along the rip current. For this, the boom walk was of great advantage. The logs were loaded with barnacles and Beebe knew that in every crevice there would be life worth investigating. Lifting one log was a slippery affair, and the use of muscle, wire hoops, boat hooks, gaffs, nets, and bags was in order. Beebe commented on the talented scientists invited to the exploration as he wondered about the fact that muscle had not been one of the requirements on their resumes. In the end, though, they mastered the lifting of the log and brought it aboard by way of the boom walk. The buckets and pans were quickly filled as the investigation of all the logs' inhabitants continued through the night.

The log was like a sieve containing fish, crabs, enormous worms that were seven and eight inches in length with tentacles, and larva, jellyfish, mollusks, single-cell animals that lit up at night. There were fifty-four different species of sea life living on that single log, a world of life floating and drifting, swept here into one monumental collection and a feast for all.

One morning, in contrast to the minutiae collected along the current, there suddenly appeared a giant squid. Will was on deck when he saw a school of white-winged butterfly flying fish. He hadn't seen them very often because they were deep-sea fish. He knew that because of the markings of lights across their bodies. Suddenly, a red squid shot up out of the water. It was after the fish, but then a very big silver hatchet fish jumped out of the water, too. It was injured. Herr Beebe said it came up from two-thirds of a mile down. And then, the thing with long arms, tentacles, shot out of the water. "A squid!" someone shouted. It was not like the octopus they'd seen previously. This one was bigger and shaped differently. Down in the water it went, then up again like a shot. Beebe said at dinner that the length of its tentacles was about eight feet, and its torpedo-shaped body about two feet long, although it was hard to tell exactly as it was coming up out of the rip. It was those tentacles that were snakelike, that reached up with big cups along its tentacles and the huge dark, oval shaped, staring eyes that were ghastly. Those tentacles reached out to the feet of the men who were watching. It was then that Will ran to the safety of the galley. He was not ready for one of the men to be wrapped up in one or two of those snakelike appendages and brought to the thing's mouth. It was one of the few times he was scared. He knew he would dream about it and relive the terror, which he did, waking up in a cold sweat. He still remembers the dream that came to him more than once.

Later, a twelve-foot hammerhead shark encircled the ship several times and they passed a section of water that was a hue of deep purple. That turned out to be a great number of jellyfish. They found schools of fish, amberjacks or yellowtails traveling in schools of tens of thousands, eggs of mollusks, anemones, purple shelled snails, salpas (deep sea fish), crustaceans (both adult and larvae), and an exciting appearance of an injured and dying hatchet fish, *Argyropeleus*, which was richly illuminated. Beebe estimated its home was about two-thirds of a mile down. On floating feathers, they found masses of ova in the number of twenty thousand on a single feather. Will read in the book that under the microscope it looked like a mass of tiny grains of rice. It was, indeed, an unbelievable harvest for study, but also for any creature that was looking for dinner. The diversity was beyond belief.

Beebe's description of sea snakes is just one of the many encounters that he wrote about in detail. *They were brilliant in color, olive green above, with many, broad, yellow cross bands, about as protectively colored as yellow daisy blossoms in a green field* (*Arcturus* 56). From the boom walk, one of these was caught in a net and hauled in. Since these snakes are highly venomous, Beebe was careful to grab it by its head and rush to the lab to place it in an aquarium. About three feet long, it had barnacles attached to its skin which must have been painful because the snake kept biting the area. While this type of sea snake cannot be out of the water for long periods of time, they are viviparous (which means they give birth to live young) and so approach land to give birth in rock crevices. One female was found with several young snakes about two feet long.

Mystery after mystery unfolded throughout the descriptions found in this exceptional harvest of sea life that were drawn from several fathoms down. Each creature was given its due. Will remembers helping to clean the lab during quiet times. There were tools to carefully record what was found, paint, paper, brushes, sculpting clay, cameras, along with scalpels, scissors, and knives used to understand the makeup of the creatures that came into the lab. An artist's attention to detail often caught more than a camera with black and white film could do in 1925. Colors were quickly recorded before the almost immediate changes occurred. Of concern also was the skeletal structure, which must be considered to understand the forever submerged life of these very small creatures.

The *Arcturus* sailed parallel to the rip current for over a hundred miles while the sun rose *on a mirror,* as Beebe described it. Here, in the calm waters of the Pacific, two great currents met and produced a wall of life. There were two warm westward streams of water with richness that challenged the imagination. By the third day of the rip current experience, the work was hectic. Besides the many buckets of sea life collected, there was the sorting and the identification of every creature no matter how small. Besides dissecting fish, accurate recordings took place by way of illustrations, photographs, maps, and soundings for measuring depths.

It is a Zoologist's Paradise, wrote Beebe.

THEY LEFT THE RIP current then, with Harry explaining that they were headed toward Darwin Bay. At this point, the *Arcturus* was halfway between Panama and Chatham, the outermost island of the Galapagos, heading in a southwest direction. They found jetsam laden with thirty-eight varieties of seeds and sprouted plants as well as sea creatures, all from the tropics, which led to Beebe's supposition that the Galapagos Islands had been vegetated by seeds and plants that had once been washed ashore. There were pieces of old ships, bamboo, pine-like wood, and palm trunks. It was these currents that brought life to the islands centuries ago.

If they had followed the rip current any further by sailing northward, they would have missed the Galapagos by about 150 miles.

Now the sky was filled with birds following the ship, which to them might have seemed like just another floating log. Will had been throwing scraps from the galley whenever an albatross came close to the ship, and now he had a bit more to give them. He was on deck at odd moments. The graceful, effortless flight of the birds was a pleasure, a sacred image not unlike that of the water along the shores of Bermuda where he would later recall that landscape time and again. The birds were companions now and feeding them brought connection, a longing, too, a unique knowledge of freedom. Although Harry said albatross ate only squid, when the birds followed the ship at various times of the day, an albatross was eager to have the scraps Will saved. It waited for him and often ate right out of his extended hand. It seemed to him its life was as lonely as his, wandering about in the ocean, the ship floating solo in the unending, uninterrupted seascape all the way to the horizon in every direction. The albatross followed him, and that it looked for him might just have been his imagination, but he didn't think so, and he still doesn't.

The Helmet

After the previous exploration on the *Noma,* Beebe's focus was always on the possibilities and wealth of information the submarine world offered. Despite the dredges and nets and hauls and all the measurements of depth and temperature, the exploration of the ocean was limited to having his feet on the deck of the ship. Diving off a pier or a boat and getting a fleeting glimpse of the world below the surface was never enough and this was monumental in his further development as a scientist, culminating in his daring deep-sea plunge in the bathysphere a half mile down, years later in 1932.

The island just ahead was called Indefatigable. There was a welcoming committee of sea birds hitching a ride along the wires and porpoises that put on a fascinating display, along with the ferocious activity of groupers that meant some fishing with rod and reel would lead to the freezer being filled. The smaller boats were put over the side and the staff headed for the white beach. There was a picnic lunch, and everyone strained to see the expected wild goats, but instead they found a big lizard under a cactus, basking sea lions, and the tracks of sea turtles that had scrambled ashore to lay eggs. It was a respite from the swaying discomfort of the days before on the Atlantic.

Now was the time. Beebe decided to try his helmet for dives deeper than he could accomplish before. The *Arcturus* was moored near the cliffs of Darwin Bay to the southeast of the collection of islands that make up the Galapagos archipelago. The summer before the expedition, Beebe had come upon a protective armored suit contraption which seemed way too cumbersome. He opted for just the helmet which was shaped like a cone and made of copper. It was made to rest on the shoulders with four ten-pound weights. All in all, it weighed sixty pounds. On the right side of the helmet there was an ordinary garden hose that was connected to an automotive air pump secured at the bow of the glass-bottom boat. The pump was operated by a long iron lever that had to be pushed back and forth. Beebe's comments about the pump included a hope that the operator at the pump would not be a daydreamer. By that he meant Ruth Rose, who was to man (or maybe that should be *to woman*) the pump operation. At the stern, a rolled-up ladder was tied in place and two harpoons were on board in case of the intrusion of a larger fish. A land line was attached to the top of the helmet for retrieval should that be necessary.

Setting off from the *Arcturus* with John Tee and Ruth Rose in the glass-bottom boat (which meant an eighteen-inch square was cut out and replaced with a square of glass), Beebe headed for the shore where there were rocky cliffs in the hope that a drop in the depths of the water would most likely mean an abundance of fish. Once overboard and in water up to his neck, Beebe kept his head dry, and the helmet was put in place by John Tee, who then added the four ten-pound weights. Sixty pounds of helmet and weights were lightened as soon as Beebe slowly submerged. If a problem arose, he knew he could simply remove the helmet and swim to the surface of the water. The helmet, simple in construction as it was, served him well throughout the expedition and no changes were made.

The helmet had two windows on the face. To prevent the danger of the windows fogging up, the surface was coated with glycerin. Since they were angled, Beebe had to look through one window at a time. These windows would hold images never seen before at depths of twenty feet or more. Beebe's hopes were high. He was ready to climb down the ladder, and when he stepped off, he was standing on the bottom.

Of that first dive at a depth of twenty feet, Beebe later wrote:

> *I sat down on a convenient rock, shut my eyes and recited my lesson: I am not at home, nor near any city or people; I am far out in the Pacific on a desert island, sitting on the bottom of the ocean; I am deep down under the water in a place where no human being has ever been before; it is one of the greatest moments of my whole life... (Arcturus 77).*

He continued later:

> *The sun's rays filtered down as though through the most marvelous cathedral ever imagined—intangible, oblique rays which the eye could perceive but no lip describe. With distance, these became more and more luminous, more wondrously brilliant, until*

> *rocks died away in a veritable purple glory. No sunset, no mist on distant mountains that I have seen, could compare with this (Arcturus* 83*).*

He made five descents in all. On the second dive, just before the helmet was put in place, the largest grey shark he'd ever seen passed by. He watched as the dark fin cut the water. It was eleven or twelve feet at least, and he watched as the dark fin cut the water close by. It was a harbinger of other sharks that might be approaching. He was aware of the fact that his unprotected limbs were exposed, yet he continued his descent.

> *Went down in about fifteen feet of water, experimenting with pressure, rate of pumping and so on. A large shark was swimming by but paid no attention to the diver. The strange beauty of the submerged scenery is hard to describe. The range of vision is limited to perhaps forty feet, while everything beyond that is wrapped in a soft luminous fog, a delicate blue haze like that of a concentrated Indian Summer, in which shadowy forms weave to and fro* (*Arcturus,* Ship's Log, April 9, 1925 398).

It was only the beginning of the exploration of ocean depths that Beebe would undertake, culminating in 1932 with the construction of a ball of steel—the bathysphere. Beebe, crunched inside and peering through a window, could observe sea life from a depth of a half mile, a possibility unknown to mankind at that time. This would become his most daring feat. But the initiation began with the helmet and the hose. Good, but not enough. Not enough for a true explorer. And maybe not enough for a writer either.

He writes about one handicap—the impossibility of writing down everything he was experiencing, hoping he could later record it all satisfactorily and in proper sequence. He never stops planning and dreaming as he writes, *This I hope to remedy in a made-to-order helmet which shall contain a cheek pouch of sorts, to hold a little writing-paper roll and a pencil, in the dry air of the side of the helmet, at the left of my face (Arcturus* 78*).*

One of his discoveries concerned the motion of the water when he submerged close to the shore. The swells of water moved the same as they did on the surface even thirty feet down. *It was so soothing, so rhythmical, that one yielded to it at times in a daze of sheer enjoyment (Arcturus* 80).

The descriptions of the various kinds of fish he encountered are seemingly endless. It was not just the colorful physical aspects of what he saw, but also the beginning of the understanding of the community of fish, how they help one another, change direction at a flash, protect themselves with all sorts of appendages and lights either to lure or escape, how the miracle of their world is that sea animals have a three-plane dimension unlike humans with only two. He thinks that the evidence of vertebrae makes a possible connection between animals on earth and creatures of the sea, and that the theory that creatures moved out of the sea to land was true.

But as he and Roosevelt had discussed, there was nothing like observing the environment in which the object of study existed.

The world below the surface of the water held a wealth of secrets in its depths.

First impressions were about the wonder of the deeper seascape, but Beebe also acknowledged the danger in one later episode when he was wearing the helmet and had submerged thirty feet down. He was at the steep slope at Tagus Cove when there was a huge swell, causing him to lose balance. He compares the incident to childhood fears as he notes:

> *I stumbled and began slowly to slide and drift out and down.... My foot struck against a coral boulder and a sea-fan gave me solid anchorage. For a minute or more I stared through the glass window—down, down at the terrible translucent blue blackness of that abyss. There would have been no quick, smashing drop as over a dry precipice in upper air, but a slow, awful rolling, with an unhasting death from cold, pressure and blackness. My reason for all this apparent personal digression is to try...to make real and vivid to the mind of the reader, the unearthliness of the depths of the sea.... (Arcturus* 341-342*).*

And in another episode, in the corals of Cocos Island where the sea was tumultuous, Beebe recorded that he was scraped and torn from the sharp edges of coral and the poisonous spines of urchins. He learned, too, that if he allowed himself to move with the flow of water, the fish began to follow him, at many points crowding around him. He saw a nine-foot shark materialize out of the blue depths. *The great, grey being, wafting along its hundreds of pounds of body by slow, gentle undulations, kept on and on until again hidden by the blue light (Arcturus* 97).

During this time of first descents, Beebe came across another grey shark at an estimated length of eleven or twelve feet. The difficulty of the moment was the fact that Beebe could not see it in full, but only through one of his helmet's two windows at a time. He could not judge distance or comprehend shape well. Was he deterred by any of these incidents? Of course not. By mid-voyage, Beebe had accomplished forty submersions and in doing so, opened that watery world to a new dimension of understanding.

He learned to bring a bit of bait with him to lure specimens that he had not seen in the nets, and to harpoon them for bringing them back to the ship where they would be rushed to the lab and inspected in several different ways. He would record the discovery, forever expanding his knowledge and that of generations to come.

WITH *THE ARCTURUS ADVENTURE* in his hands, Beebe's words bring knowledge of things Will had only guessed about during the voyage. He now has the words for proof of scenes that had formed only in his imagination. He admits that at the time he'd thought of the danger, the darkness and the sudden appearance of man-eating monsters. But now the memory becomes richer, more complete. He was jealous of David, who was allowed to make a dive with the helmet, as were several members of the staff, but that was kid's stuff. The book fills in the empty spaces.

Someone took a picture of David on deck, wearing the helmet, his expression serious as he peered out from the glass. The helmet was a quarter the length of his body. There was a photo of him standing in front of the wire shark cage that Beebe sometimes used if sharks were about. Beebe had discovered that if he flowed with the swells and didn't try to resist them by attempting to stand still, sea life usually ignored him. However, he didn't always take that chance.

For Will, then, years later, the mystery and miracle lay in the words on the page, the warped scene of what appeared outside the window of the helmet, the clarity at forty feet of distance and the fog beyond, the bright colors of the fish that his boy-self saw only in his imagination but were now shown in the photos and illustrations in the book in his lap. He remembers that David didn't mind sharing what he'd seen or what he thought, but it was never enough. They had begun talking a little. Will didn't always understand everything although he wouldn't admit it. On particularly warm nights, he remembers that they both used the hammocks on the top aft deck, their voices accompanied by the slap of the ship's hull on the water.

Words came out of nowhere. David said, "I was diving today. I only went down about fifteen feet."

"*Ja.*"

"Wish you could have come, too."

"*Ja.*"

"The fish were so many colors—red, bright orange, blue and black—one with a white cross like a belt, grey ones with yellow tails. The water plays tricks on you. You try to reach out to something believing it's within reach and you can't. It's very strange."

"*Ja.*"

"I'm writing a book about it."

Then silence. He didn't remember what David said after that because he'd talked a long time, on and on. The strange words and the gentle sway of the hammock soon put Will to sleep. Too soon, waking as the sun rose, he crept below to the galley and got ready to call the crew at *hallf pass sechs*. Dully, then suddenly, he became aware of the smell of ammonia filling the air. The ice machine had sprung a leak.

Later that morning, it was necessary to cook as much meat as possible to preserve it, and with fruit spoiling, as much of that as was possible had to be eaten. The odor of meat cooking and roasting filled the air. It was an unbearable heaven. "Help yourself," said Harry, as he cooked a little extra, some for himself and some for Will even though not all fifty-six people on board were going to have steak. Most would have soup, but Will's steak, eaten slowly in the galley after serving, was a privilege unparalleled in all his brief history.

He didn't understand why the steak reminded him of home. Maybe it reminded him of the possibilities of a home. His father was always gone, and then gone for good, never to return. His mother left him, perpetuating his fear of never having a home again. Where? Where was home?

The fish and other things they were bringing up in the nets, Will had never seen. He couldn't get close enough, the buckets being surrounded by all the scientists observing and pulling out fish to put in containers to carry to the lab. Most were too small to be looked at without a microscope. Will wondered what the scientists were exclaiming over as they hovered over the buckets and pans full of the latest catch. The first thing he did when he held *The Arcturus Adventure* in his hands was look at the pictures like a kid. Who could resist the carefully drawn illustrations, many of them filling the page although the fish were minuscule in actuality? There were a few photographs of the crew (not him) and he remembers their names, and a diagram of the ship and its lines and different kinds of nets and some of the scenery as they approached the islands, but the fish remained a mystery all his life. The fish names escaped him, too. He still can't read them and cannot even sound them out. A fish, about two inches long with eyes on top of its body. A fish with its inner fin skeleton visible outside the body. A butterfly fish with two sets of fins the colors of butterflies. A small crab that, in its larval stage, initially appeared totally transparent. A *Porpita*, a floating jellyfish. And a black fish called the little sea devil with giant teeth that were luminescent, and two appendages, one on top of its head that carried a light and a long, trailing appendage that extended from the bottom of its jaw. This fish was brought up in the Peterson trawl from a depth of four hundred fathoms. It was a fish that was quite small, about two inches or so in length, and if it was any larger, it would be the kind of thing that would have given him nightmares. There were illustrations of the scarlet-tailed triggerfish in the various stages of its color, blue to start with, then changing to grey, or purple, or yellow, red spotted under belly with blue along its spine. Its last stage was white, which was assumed to be the color just before death. All of it was recorded by the hands of artists including Isabel Cooper, Don Dickerman, Dwight Franklin, Helen Tee-Van and her husband, John Tee-Van, who was Beebe's right-hand man. The illustrations included much more than a photograph in that details were carefully drawn and included the environment in which the fish lived. It was what the artist chose to include that gave a greater understanding of the depths of the sea world.

That is exactly what Beebe and his helmet and the staff working in the lab were all about. *It seems a foolish little game when I come to write it down, but it is based on a very sound realization of a great human weakness—the contempt bred by myopic familiarity, the absolute necessity for even an artificial perspective* (*Arcturus* 76).

The Rookery

Ahead of the *Arcturus* now was Hood Island, southeast of Albemarle, the largest of the Galapagos Islands. Hood Island was of particular interest for Beebe as it was the location of an albatross rookery. Approaching the island after two days of dredging for sea life, the sight of sea lions lying on the beaches of pure white sand against the blackness of the lava rocks and coves was inviting. Beebe had once seen an albatross in the Indian Ocean and always looked for them in the southern seas of the Pacific where they were more frequent. They were rarely seen in the Atlantic, although fossil bones had been found in both England and America.

Among the scientists, no bird flight was more admired than that of the albatross. It held supremacy in the strata of winged creatures as it coasted upwind in a seemingly effortless and relaxed manner, flying into the wind, making frequent circles and intersecting spirals to reach altitude with terrific speed. They were large and heavy birds, about ten pounds despite their hollow bones, Beebe guessed, yet were well equipped for flight with ribbon-like wings that spanned from about eight or nine to twelve feet. Virtually homeless, the albatross could travel three hundred miles before landing or feeding. It was not a bird that sought the earth. It lived between sea and sky. It landed on solid ground for one reason only and that was to mate. Heading for its one ordinary business of life, the albatross seemed to sacrifice the supremacy of its breed by making the most awkward landing of any bird. On land, with a gait that often caused the bird to fall or somersault, the albatross sought this island only to carry on the continuation of its kind, a duty accompanied by an act of *tottering miserably along as if each step brought acute agony.* It seems for all its great dignity in flight the albatross was very awkward on land.

On Hood Island, Beebe was accompanied by David as well as several of the scientists. Hiking inland, he was in close contact with an albatross for the first time as a nesting bird popped out of a bush and surprised him. Beebe noted the great hooked beak of bright yellow, the white head and neck, the body freckled with grey, the dark brown wings. In flight, although the albatross appeared to be relaxed and effortless when observed from the deck of a fast-moving ship like the *Arcturus,* one could appreciate its terrific speed. But this albatross that Beebe came upon was surprisingly cooperative when Beebe pushed it aside from the nest to observe the beautiful egg. The bird remained calm. Soon Beebe was in the middle of a rookery that not only housed albatross, but gulls and frigate birds as well. In his notes, Beebe recorded three observations. One was the tremendous flight of the albatross, famous world over. The second was of the ungainly landing of the bird that he observed while on Hood, and the third was the particulars of the pre-mating dance which he considered quite beautiful and complicated.

When Beebe and David came back to the ship, they carried two albatrosses that were immediately put in cages. Seasick for a long time, the birds eventually adjusted. Of course, one of the purposes and obligations of the expedition was to collect wildlife for the Bronx Zoo, the National Aquarium, and the Museum of Natural History, but here was David, looking triumphant as he grinned at the camera, proudly holding in each spread-out arm the widely stretched out wings of one trapped and miserable-looking bird. Its fate was to live only a few months at the zoo. Beebe noted in his writings later that the albatross seemed to have no fear of man as Beebe gently pushed aside a bird that was nesting and took an egg with the bird waiting calmly to return to its nest. Beebe took the egg back to the *Arcturus* and tried it for breakfast. It was a beautiful egg. He saved the eggshell but made no comment on the taste of the scrambled egg, while Will looked on with displeasure, thinking only of the bird that could have been.

When everyone returned to the ship, Will was asked to greet them with an offering of fruit, but what escaped his lips when he looked at the caged birds was a groan. He was connected to those birds in a way he had not been connected to any human being. He remembered being horrified at the sight of the trapped birds. He would have set them free if he could. There was no life for them now. In his mind, the birds should be forever flying, forever soaring. He never forgot in odd moments throughout his life how those creatures were so cruelly cut from their purpose. They may as well have been killed, which they were, later, dying as they were made to live on solid ground. Even now, his feelings were not eased by the fact that Beebe later spoke of the public's admiration as they viewed the birds in the Bronx Zoo, but the public would never know the beauty and poetry of the birds in flight. Will was not inclined to think of poetry, but he knew what beauty was. *Schoen.* Only now, sitting in his chair in the living room on 85th Road, does he realize his good fortune in having seen the albatross in flight. In a sense, they were still his. They would live in his best memories forever. On every trip in the ten years he spent at sea, he watched for the albatross and fed them when he could. He could never describe the feeling when watching the birds in flight. It had to do with the freeing of his soul, he thought.

He remembers he teared up at the sight of the captured birds that day on the return of the men from the rookery. Tears he was quick to hide, as if his own journey across the ocean left him weeping and yet was his salvation, too.

When he could read English well enough to read some of the encyclopedia, he found out that an albatross matured at fifteen years of age. Same as him. He remembers feeling suddenly older. And stronger. His hair was growing longer, too. *Mutter* would have been shocked, but he didn't care. He knew things now. That was more important than anything else. As he looks back all these years later, he knows his strongest feelings have to do with the flight of the albatross he fed so long ago. From then on, homesickness seemed to diminish. Memories now centered on happenings, on people, and on the calm and glassy, uninterrupted sea. He was eager to learn.

Now when he relives the sight of David back on board and standing on the deck proudly spreading out the wings of the albatross so he could show the photographer how big they were, while the head of the trapped bird drooped before him, Will tries to justify it by reminding himself of the promise fulfilled by Herr Beebe to bring back to the zoo examples of the birds he found, but forgetting that at that moment and all through his young years, he disliked David, hated his privilege. But now, with the experience of his later years, he understands what he'd thought about that privilege and how it mattered less as he achieved his own place in America. There was always his work from which came a reasonable respect that had not been brought on by fear or privilege. David had had the privilege of encouragement and support and expectations, too. He didn't have to work too hard for it, or so Will thought. Will was learning that he was always free to have his own thoughts and allow himself judgements in situations he didn't like. He knew he wasn't free to say anything out loud. That was a learning, too. But in the face of the strict and confining childhood in Bremerhaven where he had learned to live in fear and dread along with an abiding self-consciousness, he was gaining confidence. His thoughts could be his. Having met David, he came to realize these many years later that it was a privilege to have known him. They had shared a life-giving experience where they could be outside of themselves and the society of their birth for a while, untethered as the albatross in flight.

The book tells him more than he could understand in 1925 with his limited English vocabulary, but what he missed he can now read in the pages. He studies the drawings and realizes a growing respect for the work of many and especially for Herr Beebe. The fact that he'd never known his father was a realization that didn't come until he was an older man reading a book.

How important knowing Beebe was, how much he admired him and still does, how he looked to him with a trust he'd never known. Maybe he had spent his life looking for a father and now realized the importance of that tattoo on his arm, his only evidence of having had one.

WHEN HE LOOKED UP *albatross* in the encyclopedia to learn more about them, he saw that the word *albatross* could also mean something that brought deep concern or anxiety. The words were all foreign and meaningless to him at the time, but later, much later, he found out *albatross* is a word used for something that gets in the way of something you want to accomplish. Maybe at the time he was so worried about what would happen to him (he was without papers) when they got back to New York, (without any papers at all!) that he kept admiring how the albatross got away and never landed anywhere except to mate. It is the song of his own life, come to think of it. Memories of the albatross and its existence in the oceanic wild bring realizations. He thinks of his own bondage on land and the obligations of family and keeping the cellar coal bin full.

There came another meaning, another word in the dictionary under albatross that fit his situation. *Encumbrance.* A burden. A trouble. A thorn in one's side. Hardship. He never believed any of it. The albatross was freedom and escape. It defined America. Maybe instead of the eagle the albatross would have been a better symbol for America. Looking back, after ten years at sea, his own landing was equally awkward except for the green lawn and the manicured bushes which were not always enough to satisfy him. Then his thoughts of escaping to the sea were still accompanied by wishful thinking and daydreams, sometimes culminating in loud threats. "I'll go back to the sea. Give it all up. Go back to the ships!" he shouted at his astonished wife.

During all those years at sea, there never was another Beebe. There had been many good men he had worked with, but Beebe he idolized, that giant in spirit who appeared in his open-collar shirt and hat, the tip of his long nose sunburned, his dark mustache, his serious and eager eyes focused to satisfy his insatiable curiosity. The dichotomy of his humor and his seriousness along with the sadness that came in waves. Will recognizes that in himself. He could be wrong. Men must find ways to save themselves and find humor and purpose, foster determined focus. He himself has too much drive, and little of the humor. Beebe had it all.

First Volcanic Sighting

The sunset was an unusual red orange, making the cliffs on the largest of the islands, Albemarle, a salmon color, burnished by the sun's last light. The *Arcturus* was near the high cliffs of Darwin Bay, closer to a very rocky coast than it should have been, which made the captain nervous. Suddenly all was quiet. Even the birds were silent. Now the cliffs of the island seemed dead, hard, bare and black as cinders, yet the sky was brilliant, signaling the end of a glorious day with a grand finale. Most of the crew had never seen anything like it, how the rays of the sun could reach and make such magic, if for only a short while as it appeared to slip into the ocean.

The coppery tinge of color in the sky remained for a long time, so long that at midnight when the second mate called a warning about it, Beebe rose from his bed and went directly to the bridge thinking what a glorious afterglow of the sunset—or maybe a burning ship. But it wasn't. "Volcano!" sprang from his lips as everyone gathered. The cliffs that hung over the ship now appeared bathed in a dim cold blue, but the orange beyond held steady. The glow was about eighty miles away, on the northern part of Albemarle. Soundings were taken at each bend in the journey as they passed the islands, names that Beebe knew well: Bindloe, Tower, Abingdon, and Indefatigable, names that would be changed in later years. Now clouds were forming and changing shape, some lit by the fires on land. Each island in the archipelago reflected the light differently over mountains and valleys, but the orange glow remained. In the night, as the *Arcturus* came closer to Albemarle Island, Beebe could distinguish separate lights, separate sources of volcanic activity.

There were two mountains on Albemarle which Beebe had previously named Mount Whiton and Mount Williams after the two men who had financed most of the *Arcturus* expedition. Between these two mountains lay a ridge from which the fiery glow emanated. Sunset-hued clouds filled the horizon at 3:00 am. As the *Arcturus* drew closer to the cliffs, the captain protested loudly about their dangerous course. Beebe then launched a small boat and headed toward the shore despite the force of the surf against the cliffs. Eventually, they found a small cove that offered access.

Later, Beebe wrote:

> *When a very wonderful thing comes into our lives for the first and perhaps last time, we betray our very birthright if we do not meet it with all the feeling and emotion and intellectual appreciation which is our human prerogative (Arcturus* 117*).*

Beebe said that volcanoes were the life blood of the planet, a kind of bursting at the seams that emits poisonous gas where microorganisms that are the toughest on earth survive. Strange to think of volcanoes as life giving but it is known that where ancient eruptions occurred, the richest agricultural soil was found years later. The birth of the islands is brought on by volcanoes where magma is trapped beneath the earth's crust and slowly escapes, falling like rain. It is the veins of lava that create islands, and in fact, all land. Volcanic rock, rich in minerals and salt, breaks down over time and is how life on earth evolves. Beebe titled the next chapter in *The Arcturus Adventure* "The Birth of a Volcano." It could be said it is the birth of life itself, and maybe all places called earth.

In 1923 in his book, *Jungle Days*, after an excursion to British Guiana, Beebe wrote,

> *A volcano in eruption and a jungle monkey—nothing can ever quite prepare our minds for the first sight of these. Neither the crude wood-cut of Vesuvius in our old school geography, nor the latest colored moving picture of Kilauea, adumbrates the awe of the silent, ascending line of smoke, or the nocturnal glow of fire, old as earth itself is old* (*Jungle Days* 166).

At night, as the crew watched from the decks of the *Arcturus*, what they saw was the entire slope of the mountain ridge lit by a string of fire from which flowed a deep red continuous and solid flame crawling to the sea as though with steadfast, evil intent. Tongues of flames shot up while steam rose from the water when the lava hit the sea. The hovering clouds reflected the inferno below. Hundreds of fumaroles, holes from which poured hot gases, grey-whitish in color, could be seen. During the day, the molten lava could not be seen as well, but at night, the volcano lit up the sky.

All through the night we steamed at half speed toward Albemarle and every hour I went up on the bridge and focussed my high-power glasses ahead. From that same indefinite glow I had seen at Tower the eruption took form and size, and at last separate, gleaming lights could be distinguished.

Not satisfied with a single wonder, Nature sometimes takes us when we are immersed in the glory of some great sight and adds unexpectedly another, an auxiliary marvel for good measure, as a hint of the overflowing richness of the cosmic storehouse. Just before dawn, when three of us were watching silently with all our eyes, a mighty shooting star struck itself alight on the rim of our atmosphere, and in a blaze of white comet-light, fell silently and accurately into the center of the lava flow. After the identical happening of last evening, this appeared more than cosmic, it seemed intentional, and for a few moments I think the state of mind of all of us reverted to that of our distant forefathers, when signs and symbols and portents regulated all of life (Arcturus 121*).*

Nothing would keep Beebe away. He would have to get to the heart of it; a dream impossible to achieve, but he would try anyway. They had difficulty finding a cove as heavy surf roiled over the half-hidden reefs. But after finding one small cove where they could leave their small boat, Beebe and John Tee-Van walked into the billowing smoke as the fires below blazed. Soon they came upon a river of smooth black lava about a mile wide that formed ripples as though it was made up of water. In reality, it was a glassy jet substance. From there, as the river narrowed, climbing became very difficult. Beebe described the sight as a cauldron, yet they climbed toward it, their distance from the volcano seeming to remain unchanged. Eventually, the heat from the lava burned their faces and scorched the bottom of their shoes. Coming upon a group of fumaroles from which gas was being emitted, Beebe experienced nausea from the carbon monoxide. Peering down one of the fumaroles, he did see the red glow of fire, something that could probably be seen at night, which piqued his ambition to hike closer and closer to the volcanic action in daylight.

He and Tee-Van lost no time in heading toward the area of smoke which lay in the middle of the two mountains. The lava flow, centuries old, made for rough hiking but eventually it was the heat of the new lava that did them in. Beebe later said it was the most difficult hike he'd ever experienced. Sitting down to take a rest was impossible. The heat on their feet was unbearable.

Lava was razor thin in some places yet some of it was still soft as they sunk into it. Their feet touched heat like the fire itself.

> *Hours of inconceivably ghastly crawling, climbing, and falling over endless miles of crumbling, sharp-edged lava, under the equatorial sun, with heat pouring over us from above and below, brought us to one of the smallest of the fumaroles, where we encountered an invisible, almost odorless gas... The journey back to shore was a nightmare. We had come close to the beginning of things* (*Arcturus* Ship's Log, April 12, 399-400).

From the mountain, Beebe saw the *Arcturus* in the sea below, appearing as a toy, insignificant in the face of what they had just seen. Continuing down the slope and onto the cove where they were to be met by one of the crew, Beebe jumped into the cool water to achieve some kind of calm. What he'd seen of the volcano burned in his memory. He would write all of it later, and when he did, he confessed no words could describe his witness to the beginnings of life itself. It happened that it was Easter Sunday, a fact he noted in the ship's log.

When Beebe and Tee-Van came back on board, they wanted nothing but eight glasses of water each and a beer. As night came on and after resting for a bit, they came back on the deck to witness the shooting star heading straight for the volcano. Beebe marveled at his good luck in seeing both the star and the volcano, as though the cosmic world was sending messages.

Will was there. He saw it, too. The star dropped right into the volcano! Was it a message? A cry went up from the crew, and applause followed. Will knew the incident was a matter of appearances only, that both the star and the volcano happened to line up each in its own vast space, but what he saw that night he'd never forget. David said, "It looks like trains of lighted cars running down the mountain side." *No,* thought Will. *It is a river of fire.* He knew then that there really was a hell like the priest at St. Panoratious said. They watched for hours. Dinner was sandwiches on the deck. No one wanted to let go of the sight that was once in a lifetime, the show that seemed to change every minute. How small they were, every one of them, in the face of such force. They all watched the lava trickle down the mountain side to Darwin Bay. To see such a beginning, to witness what few people would ever see—what was inside the earth exploding to get out—the power of it, the inexplicable force from the deep bubbling up from the sea within. Life's blood.

What if all earth was created in the same way? What if every bit of land they walked on was the result of volcanoes? The age of the earth was hidden in the layers as one dug down to find the truth. What if volcanoes were ready to explode everywhere in the ocean, shocking sailors, overturning ships, creating land that would change maps unendingly?

They watched in awed silence. The traveling fiery red and blackened snake of it, crawling down, down, and down.

On the Way to Cocos Island

First, they would have to return to Panama and obtain the badly needed ammonia, fuel and fresh water. Warm water and decaying food changed course. What Harry had told him about crossing the Equator eighteen times was probably true. Of enormous interest to Will, they also took on board limes and something called okra and other vegetables he'd never seen, and even oranges. And more bananas and mangoes, too. *Gott im Himmel.*

Docked at Panama City, David and company rode a motor car above the ancient city, once a place of extreme wealth. It was the place from which gold mined in Peru was shipped to Spain. Pirates knew it as good hunting grounds. David said so. David knew a lot, while Will, the stowaway, peeled potatoes, washed vegetables, and cleaned fish. No. He was the lucky one, with an opportunity that none of the boys in his class picture could even dream about. *Ja.* A live volcano. He was now the privileged one.

On the dock at Panama City, there was always a bag of mail delivered on board. The crew and the staff with great anticipation waited on deck. Will did, too, although he knew there wouldn't be any letter for him. Why would there be? *Mutter* probably had no idea where he was or with whom. He could have told her in a letter of his own. He would be paid at the end of the voyage. Until then, he didn't even have enough for a stamp.

Before they left Panama, one of the staff, a Mr. George Bateson, left the *Arcturus.* With him went the live animals Beebe had collected along with the two albatrosses. They were on their way to the Bronx Zoo. Will watched as the birds were carried to the dock in cages that were to be placed on a ship headed for New York. He felt their helplessness. He dared not think of returning to New York. For now, they would return to the Galapagos, and he wondered what would happen if he jumped ship and lived with the tortoises. He would have to come up with something better in July when they returned to New York. He would turn seventeen in August.

LEAVING PANAMA CITY, THEY were once again headed back to the Galapagos by traveling northwestward where Cocos Island lay about three hundred miles west from Panama. Owned by Costa Rica, Cocos wasn't exactly on the way to the Galapagos, being well north of the islands, but on the ship *Noma,* Beebe's attempt at exploration of Cocos two years ago had been thwarted by the lack of fresh water and strong currents that made any approach to the island too daunting. Now with a larger, sturdier ship, Beebe was determined to try again. It had been a long time coming.

On first sighting, Cocos seemed to be an inaccessible place with its steep high cliffs and dense green jungles. To the south of the island was Chatham Bay, where a few coves and strong currents made safe harbor a challenge. Yet legend had it that Cocos Island was frequently visited by pirates who buried booty stolen from the Peruvian silver mines that poured into Panama City. The island was often hidden behind rain clouds and because of the regular deluge, the waterfalls, of which there were many, provided fresh drinking water.

They sailed on quiet, smooth water as they approached Cocos, discovering what looked like some sort of paradise with thick vegetation, green upon green, huge palm trees that appeared fern-like, warm, humid air and soft breezes and then there were the dark, high cliffs and the prolific streams flowing from them and waterfalls that shone white and silver against the tall black lava rocks.

Will, on deck again, loved the scene before him. But now, Harry was yelling from the galley, calling *Willi* with emphasis on the last syllable which carried through the air like an alarm. Harry used the old name when he was growing impatient. It was time to help with lunch.

THE HISTORY OF THE island tells of traffic from whalers, merchant ships, and pirates replenishing their barrels. Harry couldn't stop talking about it, his eyes widening with each added segment of the stories. Will didn't understand all of it, but now the book explained it. He, of course, had to stay on the *Arcturus* while Beebe and staff and David, too, got to go off ship in the dinghies to land on the small beach and explore the island.

Harry's knowledge of the history of Cocos brought the island to life for Will. Stories of pirates and their treasure buried deep in Cocos soil fascinated him. He doubted all of it was true but enjoyed it nonetheless. He wanted to believe it. One story stuck with him about someone with a wild hope that he persisted on pursuing with the same energy as Herr Beebe. The man settled on the island with his wife in recent times and dug holes all over it but never found any treasure. He lived on this deserted island, built a home, adjusted to the strange availability of food, made his way in the unknown, and had dared to live in such a sacrificial way in the hope of riches. And what would he do with them when he found them? Would he want to leave to spend it somewhere? Brag about it? *Ja.* But he had no boat, which brought to mind the question of how this man got there in the first place. Unless he was a pirate who abandoned ship and stayed, but with a wife? Unless. Unless he and his wife were stowaways. Which meant they would always be hiding. That part worried Will. Would his own destiny always be solitary? His carefully kept secret forcing perpetual hiding?

Harry said the name: *Captain Gissler.* Later, after exploring the island with his mother, David told him that they had found deep holes which proved the story was true and that Gissler had indeed been looking for treasure during his twenty years on the island.

Will's sixteen-year-old imagination ran away with him like so many who imagined finding buried treasure. There was a whole chapter of stories about men who possessed notes and maps, now in tatters, that were passed down, claiming to reveal the locations of treasures. The name Cocos could be replaced by Treasure Island. And Captain Gissler? He had permission from the Costa Rican government which resulted in several buildings being constructed. Evidence of one or two of them could still be seen, according to David. Gissler, his wife, and the three men who worked at building and obtaining supplies and the task of digging remained for years during the time Captain Gissler cultivated bananas, coffee, limes, oranges, and vegetables. His efforts even included a small mill. Ruth Rose visited Captain Gissler in his New York home years later and wrote extensively about what and who the captain knew. He acknowledged that to his disappointment, the treasures of Cocos remained as elusive to him as they had to many men before him.

On their approach to the island, they were greeted by a great number of dolphins that raced alongside the *Arcturus*. Then came the boobies, not only the red-footed ones but green-footed ones as well. The birds discovered the poles and lines on the decks of the *Arcturus* and settled in such great numbers that the lines were packed with birds so close together they were touching each other on their roosts. Suddenly, the sky was filled with dark clouds and the scene was blurred with rain, which was followed by a brilliant rainbow. This strange island appeared to float a lonely existence in the middle of the Pacific and unlike the Galapagos, there was no record of its discovery. Maybe it had something to do with the island's disappearance behind those rainy clouds which gave the island an elusive existence. In historical maps, Cocos appeared sometimes north of the Equator and sometimes south of it.

THE RAIN ENDED. Beebe wrote:

> *At last Cocos came out fresh and green from her shroud of rain, and we slowed, sounding every few yards, drifting nearer and nearer until the heights of Nuez Island were well abeam to starboard, and Cocos itself loomed high over us .... tiny and mountainous, only about three and a half miles across, with two peaks in sight, deep-seamed with ravines, one of which was almost twenty-eight hundred feet in height* (*Arcturus* 223-224).

When the staff set off in dinghies to explore the island, they discovered that the thick vegetation was impenetrable. The only way to climb was to hike in the middle of the rocky streams. Rain throughout many months of the year kept the soil spongy where nothing ever had a chance to dry, *then a silver column of water would appear, falling from high up on the mountain, to spend itself in spray and trickle over the pebbly beach. The sun came out and the whole island glistened like a jewel with a myriad facets (Arcturus* 225*).*

Reading the book, Will sees how Herr Beebe painted with words. It was exactly as he had described. But for Will, the coming storm dominated his memory of Cocos Island, where the sky had turned black and rain advanced so quickly that the staff had to return to the *Arcturus* swiftly and only just in time. The storm developed into a gale. *The night black as ink*, he heard Herr Beebe say.

The wind must have confused the boobies, which were a mixture of tropical seabirds. They came by the hundreds, covering every surface and filling the small boats now tied on the deck. They flopped about, throwing up their latest catch of fish. The doors to the cabins and laboratory had to be closed. The staff and crew were busy grabbing birds by the wings and tossing them overboard. Many birds would just turn around and head back to the *Arcturus.* Beebe called it *The Battle of the Boobies.* At one point he tied a handkerchief to the foot of one of the birds to mark it and tossed it overboard, only to see it return immediately.

The next morning the inevitable brilliant rainbow appeared in the sky. The sea was full of dead and sodden birds, and the torrential waterfalls foamed. Will remembered the cleanup, long and tedious, as he and Harry and the rest of the crew cleared and washed the decks of hundreds of birds and bird residue. He learned a new word from Harry's lips. One could release a lot of disgust in the emphasis on consonants *sh* and *t*.

The Birthday Party, May 20, 1925

The history of Cocos Island impressed David, so it was no surprise when the theme for his thirteenth birthday was inspired by the talk of pirates. Everyone would dress as a pirate for the occasion. Harry prepared a buffet dinner and Lumpy spent two days baking and decorating a huge cake. David's mother, Dorothy, made him a pirate's costume complete with pantaloons, a red sash, a calico head scarf, a machete, rope-soled shoes and a ragged shirt. The members of the staff, always eager for a party, especially one led by their enthusiastic and fun-loving leader, Beebe himself, were all decked out in hastily assembled tattered outfits, eye patches and bandannas.

But the finishing touch for David was a cutlass, a beautiful sword from Don Dickerman, Beebe's close friend. He had named the sword Fury. It was David's proudest possession, and in the photograph in his book, his face is surrounded by the frame of a porthole, the sword grasped in his right hand, his forehead and eyebrows covered by a flowered bandanna, and a grin so wide it revealed all his teeth.

It was the transformation of Herr Beebe that was astonishing, from serious scientist to a party-loving instigator. After everyone assembled in Beebe's cabin, they marched with the accompaniment of a drum to the dining room for the buffet. Later, assembling themselves on the deck, they were smiling into the camera for a picture that appears now in the book, looking every bit like a motley crew with no clue of the expertise in science and the hard-won serious research conducted in the previous months. In the end, it was the music that thrilled Will, the appearance of mandolins and harmonicas on deck and the sound of celebration that poured into the dusk, spawned by long hard hours at sea, a scene that was the same in every direction.

Will hid behind the dinghies, listening and watching. When he was just twelve years old, he longed to play the violin and had dared to approach the music teacher who lived above the bakery in Bremerhaven about lessons. Dr. Weinmayr was his name. Will ran errands for weeks on end to pay for the lessons, but with the lack of progress, Dr. Weinmayr, beginning to suspect there was no violin at home, asked Will to bring his violin to the next lesson.

The notes on the page were ominous to Will. There didn't seem to be any connection with those notes and the music that might flow from the strings. Who knew what they were supposed to sound like? And here was Dr. Weinmayr saying, "I see you don't practice."

Will stared at him, trying to think of an answer, his heart pounding at being found out.

"You don't have a violin, do you?"

Ach. Nein.

Dr. Weinmayr pointed to the door with his thick hairy thumb and angrily said just one word, *Aus!*

Of course. What had he expected?

Which was why, on the evening of the birthday party on the deck of the *Arcturus*, Will's eyes never left Herr Beebe's hands, watching the fingers that skimmed and strummed the strings of the mandolin while his left hand pressed the strings for seconds and harmony came out. Those on deck began dancing and singing, and as unfamiliar songs to Will rang out to the star-filled night and calm waters, he watched and listened as if he were memorizing every position of Beebe's fingers. Here was the lesson. He didn't need notes on a page. He could hear the chords. They made sense as though they'd been printed on his brain before he was born. They leaned into one another as though announcing where to go on the next melody line or the next chord. He could do it. He vowed he would. It was music without the fear of having to do it according to the notes on the page. The music traveled through the evening and brought smiles to everyone. And laughter afterwards.

There were passages where the music that was part of the song flew off, free of constraints, becoming more than the black notes and lines on a page, taking an albatross flight. That was it. It was the kind of music simple enough that anyone could do it. It was so American. It included everyone. Later, the names came: "Turkey in the Straw" and "The Old Grey Mare" and "America, the Beautiful." There was togetherness and unity and joy in the air as the notes and voices flew over a calm sea and rose into the warm air of a night in the tropics, to be lost somewhere in an empty sky—a thing or spirit apart from them but part of them, too. He never forgot it. The feeling comes back whenever he plays "Turkey in the Straw" in his own kitchen with his cigarette still burning in the glass ashtray, as he nods his head in a gesture of *yes* at the end of each song, then tapping the harmonica on his knee and feels pretty damn well satisfied.

That William Beebe. A man of many dimensions. Focused, he was obsessive about his research, but something of the artist held sway in him, too, between his descriptive writing and his music, and the joy of partying fun. God bless him. A man could be many things all at once.

Our Islands

Beebe and some of the crew, including Ruth Rose and Bill Merrium, anxious to put their feet on solid ground after weeks at sea, were eager to explore one of the small islets south of Gardner near Hood Island. The shores of these islands were covered with coves, peninsulas, pinnacles, and caves, but the landscape was covered with vegetation as in a newborn land. They chose the island that had high cliffs and high boulders of black rock. The surge of waves withdrawing from the rocks revealed bright sponges, starfish, and anemones on those black walls, and incongruously there was also a tree blooming yellow.

After pulling the boats on shore, they climbed the rocks to find a colony of sea lions. Ruth Rose talks about wanting to be accepted in sea-lion circles. She writes *sea lions are nice people*, and as she walks among them, discovers that the very young had something wrong with their eyes. One appeared to be completely blind and so was taken to the *Arcturus* for examination. It was conjunctivitis and medication was given. Ruth Rose mentions the concern for all the other pups on the island.

As they continued the hike, they were surrounded now by high rock walls that revealed a cave-like low arched opening. They crawled in. Despite the fact there was no roof, and that it was still daylight, darkness surrounded them. They were in a large chamber where the sounds of the sea lions, and one that seemed to be *granddaddy of them all*, escaped by climbing what looked like a chimney. The sounds of soft hissing by the sea lions surrounded them and the calls of the birds added to the mysteriousness of the cave. As they climbed higher, there was suddenly a white plateau gleaming in a ray of sun. From there they could look down the vast drop of about a hundred feet to the sea.

> *We sat on the brink of the precipice and with heads tilted far back, watched a frigatebird soaring overhead. There was something hypnotic in the unceasing song of the wind, the abyss below, and the vast blue vault above, empty save for a pair of outstretched wings that rocked lazily round and round a wide circle. At long intervals those wings flapped twice, then stiffened and held motionless, while the bird, confidently cradled on the rushing air, swung in its chosen orbit and watched its world....*

> *Sometimes, in the confusion of cities, in the midst of the dirt and noise and countless irritations that make civilization seem a deplorable blunder, it is good to remember that a frigatebird is winging over that little secret harbor which, it may be, was never*

> *seen by any other human eyes than ours* (*Arcturus* 169).

They christened the island Osborn Island for Professor Henry Fairfield Osborn, who was president of the Natural History Museum and head of the New York Zoological Society. He was the professor who recognized the promise of a young Beebe.

From the cliff on Osborn, they had a view of an islet that was even smaller. The temptation to explore it was imminent and fulfilled. A few examples of entomology were taken but for the most part, the Galapagos offered a narrow field as far as species were concerned. Still, those collections were sorted and preserved for future study. Volcanoes made land, and even the smallest living thing on it, made soil, and before any human witnesses were around to take note, there was mutation after mutation. Beebe knew that, and much of his work was about proving Darwin right. Mutations are multiplying even as these words are written.

Now in his chair in the Cape Cod on 85th Road, Will realizes a surprising thing. He finds he likes to read. In the hours after supper and sometimes far into the night, sitting in his chair in the small living room, he reads with the dictionary at his side, telling the kids to *shush*, which they do. Their father is reading.

He remembers it all, the huge cliff that looked more like a city high-rise jutting out from a small unnamed island in the middle of the Pacific, when the small boats were put down and many of the staff left. He would have loved to go, too, but the dishes in the sink waited. Lumpy, the baker, gave each member of the expedition some coffee cake he'd just pulled out of the oven so they could have a breakfast picnic. Will took care of the leftovers, his reward for cleaning the bowls and pans. Life was good.

A Shire of Water

On May 24, 1925, on the east side of Chatham Bay, sixty miles south of Cocos, Beebe found what he called an island of water and named it Station 74. He'd travelled thousands of miles but the challenge now was to explore in a more specific way. Here, the Arcturus would float mid-ocean for ten days, sometimes unanchored, and that column of water that he supposed existed within the circle of cerulean blue would reveal its contents and relationships. This was research considerably narrowed and focused.

> *I wanted to learn all I could of what flew in the air, floated on the surface, dived in the depths or burrowed into the substance of this tiny pin-point in the great Pacific (Arcturus* 321).

Again, it was the helmet that offered access to the coral reef and opened an opportunity for ever deeper exploration. Before he descended, Beebe described his sighting of far-off Cocos Island:

> *What I saw as I looked around above water just before I dived was a sort of upground, I know of no other word—the beautiful, great bay with the Arcturus riding at anchor, while high overhead rose the steep mountain slopes of Cocos, covered with dense, green jungles—tall palms and graceful, lace-like tree-ferns standing out above all the rest, while fig trees clung to the steepest slopes, dropping down perfect portières of dangling rootlets. In and out, like a warp of silver threads among the green foliage, shone the waterfalls—the glory of all this island loveliness, dozens of them, slipping down from rock to rock or sliding gently over hundred-foot stretches of emerald moss* (*Arcturus* 299).

Once the island of water was decided on for focused research, Beebe began with the study of species of birds flying above the *Arcturus* and included the meticulous gathering of unknown and known species in the skies as well as evidence of traveling seeds and eggs and insects gathered on logs or feathers. Added to this was the sight of swimming reptiles, snakes and turtles. Musing on the possibilities of a desert island in the process of *accidental populating*, Beebe notes that *the simple beginnings of the struggle for existence between seed and seed, animal and animal, justifies serious study and explanation as to the variances on land* (*Arcturus* 333).

> *So even with the scattered and imperfect observations which I was able to make, I could see my island stocked with plants and insects, shore fish, crabs, sea turtles and birds, the whole numbering over four hundred individuals (Arcturus* 338*).*

He began with the recording of birds flying overhead and then concentrated on what floated on the surface of the water in as small an area as possible and finally, what existed in the depths—much farther down. In his writing, Beebe carries the idea further:

> *The earth is altering with eldritch rapidity before the onrush of increasing numbers and the destructiveness of mankind. The details of early evolution and the clarity of primitive relationships are daily becoming less distinct, more complex (Arcturus* 338*).*

Mutation, then, is continuous.

DESCRIBING THAT COLUMN OF water that Beebe referred to as a shire was an adaptation from the British concept of county or section. He describes its presence by the color of the water, a ring of blue like none other he'd experienced, a mark of the column he notes as a complete community of fish life amongst the coral and beyond.

For his descent, the weight of the helmet was changed to seventy-five pounds. It is in his description of the coral itself as he descends the rope ladder that Beebe veers into language that fires the imagination. He notes,

> *I am eclipsed, and change planets,* and as he descends further, he describes not only a *city of giant mushrooms,* but also *a boulevard of the whitest sand, a palace of the Dalai Lama,* and *a fairy replica of the temple of the Tirthankers at Benares. Then a cloud of pagodas filled the end of the sandy vista, silhouetted against the blue at which I can never cease marvelling whenever I think of this water world,—a pale cerulean, oxidized now and then with the glimmering through of some still more distant monument* (*Arcturus* 300).

Fish in this environment live in an order that Beebe likened to that of human life in community. He also describes the challenge he had in recording all the activity surrounding him as a *twenty-ring circus.* He carefully observes the castes of the Nomads and the Grazers, the former being the zeppelins that hunt in singles in mid-water and are mainly sharks, giant rays, and groupers, and include the slow yellow-eyed grey shark (about four to nine feet in length), the white finned island shark who is a scavenger looking for dead or crippled creatures, and the not to be trusted, curious tiger sharks, which can be thirty feet in length. These have no home, as many other fish have.

The Grazers, however, nibble on the life in the coral, keeping well fed on algae, worms, shells, crabs, and other growths. They are the yellow-tailed surgeons that are well protected by the poisonous spines on the exterior parts of their bodies and their ferocious teeth of varying shapes such as chisel- or splinter-like.

The two castes which seem to be Beebe's favorite are the Squatters, those who dwell in temporary homes in the coral, and the Villagers, who have their own domiciles. It is here, observing ninety different species of fish over many hours in the same vicinity or community, that Beebe admits his own inadequacies in the study and description of fish. The dependency of certain fish on other fish was a remarkable insight and discovery, and reinforced the idea that creatures had to be studied in the environment that was theirs.

There was so much more information coming to light than could ever be revealed by creatures brought up in the trawls. The challenge, of course, lay in Beebe's tireless determination in probing the strange world of the ocean and translating it in terms of human thought and creative prose. It is the combination of scientist and writer that reaches out to the reader, popularizing an unknown world that people needed to learn about and understand.

AS THE *ARCTURUS* CIRCLED the island of water and hauls from five hundred to eight hundred fathoms were gathered every one hundred feet, the dredges continued to scrape the ocean floor. The adaptation that sea life had to make at every level was obvious. As per Beebe's careful recordings, the yields of 3,776 fish contained 130 different species.

During Beebe's exploration of the shire of water, his own fear of ocean depths become evident despite his eagerness to descend a half mile down in a bathysphere years later. Measurements taken at this location of the shire at seven hundred and seventy-one fathoms resulted in the name, Station 74. The desire to explore greater depths was always part of Beebe's plan, something he was able to achieve much later in 1932. Yet it was a fearful undertaking as well.

With the absence of light, there is no plant life at the lower depths of the ocean. There is only the violet blueness of moonlight, lower temperatures, and the weight of the water. On descending further, the blackness is absolute and the pressure on surfaces is over a ton per square inch. Deep-sea life lives out its existence in eternal silence and blackness. All deep-sea life is carnivorous, and much of it bears illumination. When fish are injured, gases release and they are subject to "falling upward" toward the surface of the water, offering a feast for birds and other fish. The surprising thing that happened in the lab aboard the *Arcturus* was the powerful illumination of a deep-sea creature that could light up the whole darkroom, with light that lasted for almost two hours.

The discovery of blindness in certain sea life also reveals evidence of bright illumination. In some fish, although eyes are present, they appear to be useless. However, pectoral fins are split into what might be considered fingers, enabling these fish to find food, mate, and avoid danger. Illumination allowed small edible creatures to be lured.

The trawls brought up deep-sea life that lived three-quarters of a mile down, and what was pulled up was a mass of *pale salmon jelly*. When disintegrated with water, the mass looked like it was made up of glass and jewels, but it was plankton, Beebe noted. And the result was the appearance of thousands of minute organisms whirling in the pan, specimens of jelly fish, sea-worms, shrimp, and tiny copepods.

WILL SAW THE HAUL from the deep sea. In the photo of Herr Beebe pouring over the tubs of sea life pulled up in the trawls, the specimens were small and were sorted by six of the scientists into categories of six different species. It seemed so undramatic. Yet Beebe's explanation in the text and some of the photos of a few fish reveal that sea life like the pallid-white pelican fish, in coping with extreme pressure and darkness, have a *great cavernous maw*, and the silvery thread eel has *unbelievably thin and curved, wire-like jaws (Arcturus* 360).

In deeper water, the red light of the sun finally disappears altogether and so does plant life. With the appearance of small fish with huge mouths and greatly distended bodies that contained their last meal, there was proof that deep-sea life is completely carnivorous. Tooth and claw is survival. Drawings of specimens from the deepest hauls of the nets at six hundred fathoms revealed the sea devil fish with appendages that were finger-like and the brotulid fish with no appendages at all. From a depth of five hundred fathoms appeared the pelican fish with a huge head and mouth but body as slender as a snake. This fish could consume a much larger creature with that mouth and with a body that was distensible enough to accommodate a large meal.

Exploration that had nothing to do with hundreds of fathoms but rather twenty feet with the diving helmet was far more dramatic. At this point, Beebe had made at least forty submersions with the helmet. His ladder of descent at ten feet changed alternately to twenty feet and proved the presence of rip tide and swift current. He could see to a range of about forty feet, he said. Diving in what he called a ring of water where the coral reefs grew in strange and colorful splendor, a white-finned shark appeared. It was followed by fifteen more. The ladder to the small boat that was waiting for him was twenty feet above him as he crouched between two coral growths for protection. The sharks did not appear to be curious about him. He attempted to walk forward with the hose from the dinghy above trailing behind him. Now it was a tiger shark that weaved slowly toward him. In his fright, Beebe judged it was thirty feet long. In a few moments he calmed down enough to consider the comparison between this shark and the ones he had just seen and came to a better judgment of eighteen feet. He says, *The great elasmobranch came on until I could see the black veins in its yellow, cat-like eyes, and the loose, adenoid-gape with its lining of triangular teeth. The mighty tail swept farther to one side, the shark veered—and passed* (*Arcturus* 218). Beebe tells how he made his way to the bottom rung of the ladder and hung there for a while, collecting himself. Rising to open air, he ends the story with these words, *with a gasp of wonder at it all.*

HIS CIGARETTE BACK IN the ashtray, Will looks up *elasmobranch* in the dictionary that he keeps handy at his side and discovers it means *any of the subclass of cartilaginous fishes that have five to seven lateral to ventral gill openings on each side that comprise the sharks, rays, skates and related extinct fishes* (Webster's).

Elasmobranch. Imagine knowing a word like that. And *cartilaginous*, too. *And an eighteen-foot shark*. Imagine terror and panic reduced to *a gasp of wonder*.

But later, he reads the following account written by Beebe and imagines him safely in his New York apartment working on the manuscript for publication in 1926, where he says:

> *As long as my book-and-legend fear of sharks dominated, I saw them as sinuous, crafty, sinister, cruel-mouthed, sneering. When I came at last to know them for harmless scavengers, all these characteristics slipped away, and I saw them as they really are—indolent, awkward, chinless cowards. They are to a barracuda as a vulture to an eagle; a ladyfish has a thousand times less weight and double their courage* (*Arcturus* 303).

Quite a different view, thinks Will, when the actuality is thought about in the safety of one's own living room in a posh apartment on the upper west side of Manhattan. He was human, that Beebe, like all of them, but with an extra dose of optimism and curiosity.

Narborough Island, Biggest Fish

They were just north of Narborough Island when the *Arcturus* was surrounded by three devilfish or rays or sunfish, the monsters of the sea. It was the same fish but with varying names. What could be seen from the bridge or the crow's nest were fish the approximate size of a barn door. To Will, it was the most exciting event of the expedition. Three of the staff set out in a rowboat with the idea of harpooning one of them. They were fortunate to have missed the powerful wing tips of these big rays or the boats would have been flattened into the sea.

One of the rays, successfully harpooned, was their focus now. It was just a matter of letting it tire out, which took the better part of two hours. The fish was shot and harpooned several times. A trail of blood followed the captured ray, which was then towed to the ship and hauled onto the deck.

This fish would not be taken to the lab and disappear before Will's eyes. It was a fish the men walked on top of and around, taking care to stay away from its mouth which was four feet wide. From wing tip to wing tip it was eighteen feet. It was weighed by cutting off chunks and weighing them, then multiplying that number by the width of the fish. It weighed 2,310 pounds. Its liver weighed as much as a man. And there was a baby ray, or devilfish, that weighed twenty-eight pounds with a fin spread that measured three and a half feet. The baby would be preserved and brought back to the New York Zoological Society. There were numerous parasitic fish attached to the mother's body in the number of thirty-eight or so. Some of them fell off when the ray was lifted from the water. The devilfish nearly covered the whole deck.

The scope of sea life, from monster size to the minute and transparent larva stages of crustaceans, is mind boggling. Big fish and fish you could eat was what common knowledge of the water had always been about as far as Will was concerned, especially in the sea along places like Bremerhaven. But from the ocean depths were creatures that adapted themselves to little-known worlds in conditions so foreign that it makes Will wonder if mankind would also be capable of adapting to situations that were unforgiving. Except for war. One could never get used to war. The mass destruction mankind does to itself.

THE DECK HAD TO be washed. Scrubbed, actually. The aftermath brought a bit of sorrow, too. The magnificent fish just had to be harpooned, and finally shot, didn't it? How else would you know about it? Still... Wanting to read about the devil fish, he had skipped ahead in the book where there was a photograph of the ray lying on the deck with crew members stepping wide over the huge flaps of its fins now extended in surrender, its underside pale in the newness of sunshine.

The devil fish was caught on June 11, toward the end of the expedition. They would be in New York at the end of July. In all the happenings on this journey, it was the devil fish that was the most remarkable. It was the first story he told to guys at the shop, details of the size now exaggerated to monster size and unimaginable to those who'd not been there to see it. He so enjoyed the story of the giant ray, the great impossibility of it, the hidden horror in the depths of the sea lying on the deck, how its length and width gave inaccurate accounts of weight as it was cut up in one-foot pieces to be weighed and the amount multiplied. The baby ray, weighing in at almost thirty pounds, was sent to the zoological society in New York. He told the story many times in the bar on 86th Street that he frequented before he got married. The eyes of his friends widened, even though he was sure they thought it was just another fisherman's tale. He wanted to tell them that knowledge was in the details but didn't want to be a smart aleck. Those details surprisingly mattered so much. You can't care about what you don't know. The details carried something sacred, like truth, an indisputable truth.

But the ray's struggle and capture stuck in his mind all these years as a kind of grand finale to the expedition, the fight for life being so strong. And too, the determination and persistence of the men in the capture. Who would win in the end, in the struggle between the ocean and the men now scouring it? Here were men with guns and boats and ropes and knives and harpoons while in the midst of all the shouting Will could see the sunray's fight for life. In the end, there was the shouting and the excitement over the battle and the winners with flushed faces clapping each other on backs wet with sweat enjoying a victory.

Was that it, really? What did they need to know about a fish so mighty? Was it just the fact that it was there to be conquered? The dragon from the sea, its mere size an invitation to kill?

HE THINKS OF AN incident aboard a tanker he'd been on in later years. It leaked oil, leaving rainbows of color floating on the surface, surely killing anything in its way, especially the plankton. Especially the kind that lit up the surface of the water where the oil would be deadening food, eliminating oxygen, killing stardust and its generations to come. Deep down, he fears the thing that is driving modern man to conquer. But maybe not. The oceans being so vast, with unimaginable depth. Maybe not.

The Volcano Revisited

Nine weeks after the first sighting of the volcano on June 14, they were on the way from Panama City where the supply of fuel and fresh water was replenished. They crossed the Equator yet again and passed the northeastern shore of Albemarle, the largest of the Galapagos Islands, where they caught sight of the still active volcano. New wonders were to be discovered as the lava hit the sea.

Will had just served a breakfast of pancakes when the foghorn sounded from the bridge. As luck would have it, the *Arcturus* was in the same vicinity as when they first visited the volcano. Everyone left breakfast and ran to the deck. Herr Beebe climbed to the crow's nest in fierce wind. He reported a surface of deep blue water about five miles off the coast of Albemarle. They sailed back and forth four times to get as close to the island as they dared. It seemed to be another rip tide but in actuality, it was due to extreme changes in the temperature of the water.

Lava had been working its way down the slope toward steep cliffs. Nine cascades of molten rock gushed from the face of the black coast and dropped into the sea where columns of steam were blown by the strong winds. Huge pieces of cliff crumbled under the pressure and crashed outward to release fresh torrents of red-hot lava. There were explosions as the lava, so rapidly cooled, could be seen now as the rocks glowed above the breakers. They could hear the hissing and rising of steam as waves hit the shore. Along the coast, the water was light green because it was heated by the lava. A clear line marked the beginning of the deep blue which was the cooler ocean water.

All hands were on deck now watching the lava crash into the sea. It was a phenomenal sight that few get to witness. The *Arcturus* crossed the line and when it did, Herr Beebe said the bow of the *Arcturus* was in green water where the temperature was ninety-nine degrees while the stern was in blue water where it was seventy-eight degrees. They circled four times about five miles offshore, crossing that line again and again, accompanied by great clouds of steam. It would have made a great painting, the blue sky, the black cliffs, the red lava, the white steam, the green water close to shore and the cerulean blue of the cooler ocean. The photos in Will's album are black and white, of course, but the colors were unforgettable. He cannot imagine that such a sight is possible to put into words. Yet here it is in Beebe's book.

THEY PASSED THE ISLANDS then. He hoped he would remember the names when years later, many of them were changed. In 1925, they were James, Bindloe, Indefatigable, Tower, the Daphnes, Eden and Albemarle. The Galapagos Islands are now famous as a tourist destination.

End of June

The steering gear and dispenser on the *Arcturus* were out of commission and fresh water was nearly depleted, which meant another Equator crossing as they headed to Panama City for repairs and supplies. It was also time for Dorothy Putnam and David to disembark the *Arcturus* and board another ship bound straight for New York, along with specimens that Beebe was sending back to the New York Aquarium and the Bronx Zoo. David, bags packed, appeared on deck and shouted out, "Where's Will?" and when Will appeared from the galley, David, smiling wide, saluted him. Will saluted back. He couldn't think of anything to say, so he called out, *Hallf pass Sechs!* which made David laugh. "Vant some zoop?" he added. He had made a friend on this journey. They were about to return to their very separate worlds, never to be in touch again.

Harry said they would soon head to the Sargasso Sea for another look, which meant another passage through the canal, the short cut and a long cut, come to think of it—reminding Will about all that hard work and death from malaria, and Roosevelt's "on with it" determination. The canal was a miracle, a planning made perfect after many failures. America did that. It must have been such an honor to be a part of that work, overcoming the challenges of nature and being a part of something that would make a big difference. Instead of fighting in war for power and with hate, there was this canal that helped everybody all over the world. Real work made everyone reach for good, gave purpose and light. It was the antithesis of war. He was to go through the canal many times over the ten years he was on the ships, but he never tired of seeing it.

The volcano has stayed with him all his life, too. It was a fury worse than what men could ever produce, he thought at the time. It was a shocking fury that was good, that needed time to birth an island, the light from which good things flowed toward a kind of eternity, that gave us earth. Dare we think of that as an eternity? Or of the existence of God? Somebody in charge?

Yet now, after another war, there is the nuclear bomb. It was a fury made by man but a necessity, they said. As for him, he isn't so sure. It was another manmade hell. He says this to no one. Anxious for World War II to end, his neighbors wouldn't agree. He understands their helplessness, waiting for sons to come home.

The Hudson Gorge

Repairs completed at Panama City, water and coal replenished, they approached heavy winds in the Caribbean with the ship plowing into the sea with alarming nose dives. There was some *sargassum* now, although it was in thousands of small pieces that were not fresh. Much of it that had been brought aboard showed nothing more than dead fish. Plowing through those same rough seas, Beebe introduced reading-aloud-with-discussion-parties in the evenings as they waited for calmer seas.

During those evenings, Will and Harry recalled some of the food that Will had been introduced to during the previous months. With Harry's help, he named croquettes, okra, limeade, fried banana, chocolate, roast and stewed chicken, stewed fruit, boiled rice, mangoes, bananas, cocoa, lime, squash, custard and biscuits with jam. Will wondered if he would ever taste them again. They didn't name the fish especially, but grouper was his favorite. At one point after having hauled in a shark, Harry fried the meat for lunch. Herr Beebe and a few others were okay with it, but most of the crew refused even a taste.

They passed Cuba and Haiti, saw sheets of lightning in the evenings, gathered more *sargassum* that was mostly decayed.

There was a slight increase in new, pale, freshly grown *sargassum* which did not yield much in the study of fish. Again, the Sargasso Sea was an unyielding disappointment. One of Beebe's wealthiest sponsors, the man who had provided the yacht now called the *Arcturus,* Henry Whiton, would be disappointed as he was most interested in researching the Sargasso Sea and hoped study of it would be the main focus of the expedition. They were close to New York City now. Attempts to see the Sargasso Sea at its prime had been thwarted. There was no sight of *vegetation so thick it stopped ships from movement*, as Columbus had written about. Once again it was not to be. In compensation, Beebe decided to investigate the Hudson Gorge, a deep canyon about a hundred miles from the heart of the city. Beebe hoped the gorge would reveal evidence as important as the rest of the expedition, especially as it was so close to the city. And indeed, it did.

As they neared New York City, there was no sight of land, even though the city was only an hour away by plane and a day by sailing. With that in mind, the crew got ready the 180-foot pennant which would be unfurled as they drew closer to New York. One hundred eighty signified the number of days of the expedition. The *Arcturus* was now heading to the Hudson River Gorge and according to the sounding wire put down, the depth was now six hundred fathoms. They were at the edge of the continental shelf.

The Hudson River Gorge spans a width of seven and a half miles and is more than two miles deep in some places. It has been submerged since the Pleistocene epoch a million years ago. At that time, the level of the ground was a half mile higher than it is now. Flood waters from the Hudson fed by four tributaries, the

Connecticut, the Housatonic, the Passaic and the Hackensack Rivers flowed to the Atlantic. Because the Palisades were four times higher than they are at present, there was good reason to believe that this might have been the site of the highest waterfall in the world. The Hudson flowed into a canyon that was larger than any known to man at the time, including the Grand Canyon.

It is now known that the Mariana Trench in the western Pacific is the largest canyon at 36,089 feet deep, a nearly seven-mile depth. It is crescent shaped, and about 1,580 miles long. Deep-sea science is now accomplished with remote controlled vehicles and human occupied submersibles.

However, one hundred years ago, Beebe's sounding wire reached the bottom of the Hudson Gorge at 2,800 feet, requiring almost a mile of wire to reach the bottom, a startling revelation at the time. The *Arcturus* was floating over the deepest part of the gorge, where hundreds of species such as sperm whales, sea turtles, and deep-sea corals sought cooler temperatures as ocean temperatures increased. Beebe says, it was *a region eternally cold, with ultimate silences, and darkness and pressure beyond all human imagination (Arcturus* 368).

They put in all the nets: the Otter trawl, forty feet long with a gaping mouth, and the Peterson trawl, and then at intervals, other nets which were towed from depths of three to five hundred fathoms. For four days and nights, the trawling and dredging was constant, the abundance of the yield, huge. In addition to the netting, the harpooning of fish from the pulpit was also very productive. Sharks not normally seen so close to Manhattan circled the *Arcturus,* showing white fins above the water. Dolphins and small whales swam by, and thirty-two new and rare species of fish were hauled from the deep sea. The desire to design a way for a human to travel deeper than ever before and observe creatures in their habitat was growing stronger. The sea life Beebe found was typical of that appearing in other deep seas, and as expected, many organisms had died as soon as they faced the greatly reduced pressure. Beebe's desire to accomplish deep-sea diving was all he could think about.

Interesting to note, sailing now toward the great temples of civilization in New York City, Beebe records in the ship's log debris from the city:

> *Rubber nipple from a baby's bottle, cardboard milk-bottle tops, empty milk of magnesia bottle, cans, leg of a rubber doll, piece of a bathtub, and a large wooden spigot.*

Aside from that, among the abundance of life gathered and new to science, Beebe took in thirty-two kinds of deep-sea fish which were included in a collection of 768 specimens at three or four hundred fathoms, while larger black species came from five or nine hundred fathoms. They were delicate, with lights along their bodies and enormous mouths. Among the small gathering of *sargassum* was a small trigger fish that changed color many times to the frustration of the illustrators. Beebe wrote,

> *This little Joseph of the sea was one of my greatest delights, and in his scant two inches I saw and*

> *respected what...typified fearlessness, dignity, poise, adaptation, besides incredibly kaleidoscopic beauty* (*Remarkable Life* 259).

From the blackness of depths under four hundred fathoms were found lantern fish with scarlet or green eyes, with stomas and huge mouths and sinister teeth that were common to other species only found in tropical waters. These were findings that gave rise to articles, donors, and exhibits at the Bronx Zoo and the New York Aquarium, and the swell of interest in preserving the Galapagos Islands. The inspiration for scientific papers about the islands and the Hudson Gorge were carried out until the mid-1940s. Henry Whiton must have been pleased as Beebe had fulfilled his promise.

The National Oceanic and Atmospheric Administration is pursuing designation of Hudson Canyon as a National Marine Sanctuary.[1] It is known to be two miles deep in some places and seven and a half miles wide. President Biden's plan announced in 2022 was to safeguard critical habitat threatened by devel-

1. For background and timeline see https://sanctuaries.noaa.gov/hudson-canyon/

opment and global warming by conserving 30 percent of the nation's land and waters by 2030.[2]

One night at the end of July, the sky grew cloudy, making the evening a good one for plankton, the collection of organisms that love darkness and stay far below the rays of the sun and moon. Surprisingly, plankton approached a search light that was concentrated in a small area, swimming in and out of the variations of light. It was a fitting end as the *Arcturus* sailed toward the New York Harbor and a grand finale to its adventure.

Then, all too soon, the packing and dismantling began. Suitcases were pulled out of storage and formal clothes reappeared and were unfolded. The trappings of modern life were eyed with a certain amount of sighing. On July 30, the *Arcturus* headed

---

2. *According to a June 8, 2022 report in* The Washington Post, *the marine sanctuary near one of the most densely populated areas of the Northeast U.S. would connect diverse communities across the region. "I am excited about how this amazing underwater environment can inspire shared interest in conserving our ocean," said Rick Spinrad of the National Oceanic and Atmospheric Administration. It was agreed among the leaders in the NOAA that the sanctuary could become vital for sea life seeking cooler temperatures. Over 200 species of ocean life were noted as well as coral sponges judged to be more than 1,000 years old. Today, canyon explorers have documented corals covered in plastic and other debris.*

for the dock at 81st and North River with the giant pennant billowing and waving in the breeze. Beebe says, *Every ship on the way saluted us, from garbage scows to big liners, and as courtesy required that we answer every blast, we had barely steam enough to creep up to the pier* (*Acturus*, Ship's Log, 425).

To people around the harbor and at the dock in New York, the *Arcturus* must have been a grand sight with its 184-foot pennant and flags flying from every wire accompanying the horns and whistles filling the New York air. Will, waving from his place on the third deck, realized for the first time the importance of the expedition. The recognition in New York of Beebe's accomplishment was followed by the appreciation of the work with the publication of his book, *The Arcturus Adventure,* in 1926. It was an immediate bestseller.

It took a few more days of hard work to disassemble the galley and beyond. Will got to see the Statue of Liberty this time in full daylight. His future was blank for the moment and worries over the great uncertainty descended on him again, with a whole boatload of sadness, too. Harry had a few words for him: "Behave yourself, mon. You did good. Hope you learned something!" To which Will said, "*Ja.* I can count now and know how to make fried bananas!" Harry merely shook his head and said softly, "Good luck!"

Herr Beebe smiled and shook Will's hand. "What an adventure, eh? *Auf Wiedersehen,* young man."

The word, *Danke*, was not enough but it was the only one that could leave Will's lips just then. He'd wanted to say more but couldn't utter another word. As always, Beebe looked him in the eye and said, *Nein. Danke schoen to you!*

His uncle waited on the pier, just as he had done when Will first walked up the gangplank. Will had his pay envelope in his pocket, a secret he would share with no one, the beginning of a slavish life of saving money he never could overcome. Uncle Helmut took him back to the apartment in Brooklyn, reminding him to take note so next time he could find his own way. At home with *Mutter* and Lieschen, he had so many things to tell with some English words thrown in.

In a week and a half, he would be seventeen. Mutter said, *Gott im Himmel. Wie gross Sie sind*! (How big you are!)

At a pawn shop, he bought a second-hand guitar with only one string missing and at Kleins on the Square, a jacket that fit. At the apartment in Brooklyn, he had to sleep on the floor as a man and his wife, also "come overs," had arrived at the apartment in his absence. They were legal, though, and no threat. In a few days, Uncle Helmut showed up again, blasting the door open with a raucous, *Wie gehts!* (How goes it?) and announced a job for Will on another ship. He was to report to the dock in the morning, the beginning of an unplanned decade at sea, while on land later, the Depression descended. As for Will, working on the seas during that ten-year period meant he always had a job and he was never hungry again.

He followed Beebe's expeditions and studies through the years. Beebe was often in the news and his work remained in the public eye through articles in *The New York Times* and *The Na-*

tional Geographic. It was in the *Geographic* issue of June, 1931, in an article called, "A Round Trip to Davey Jones's Locker," that there appeared evidence of the celebratory culmination of the long mulled-over idea of deeper ocean diving than anything accomplished before. The article contained colorful, detailed paintings of deep-sea life by Edith Bostelmann and photographs of the bathysphere being lowered into the sea carrying Beebe and the creator of the bathysphere, Otis Barton. It was a major triumph. Will saved the issue and placed it next to his album of photos from the *Arcturus* and his copy of *The Arcturus Adventure* in the bottom drawer of his dresser, along with other treasures like his citizenship papers, the picture of the boys in his school, and his Machinist Union membership card.

In May of 1928, he learned that Beebe had been granted an honorary Doctor of Science degree from Tufts University and a Doctor of Letters from Colgate. Beebe was now officially Dr. Beebe as his crew and people who worked at his side had been calling him for years.

The Bathysphere

It is 1926. Back in the City, Beebe begins writing *The Arcturus Adventure.* His previous books, such as *The Log of the Sun, Edge of the Jungle, Jungle Days,* and *Galapagos: Worlds End* (this last written after the expedition on the *Noma* in 1924), were selling well, as would the coming book. Articles in *The Atlantic Monthly, The Bulletin* (Bronx Zoo), *The Ladies Home Journal, Vanity Fair,* and *The New York Times* kept him in the spotlight.

The city, as people call New York as though it was the only city in the world, can be a rather insular place, as Beebe says in the *Unseen Life of New York:*

> *New York City, to several million of us, is the focus of the universe... Like cave men of old we clamber up to our little cubicles, tunneled out of the street canyons, there to be happy or miserable, successes or failures, to live and to die* (*Remarkable Life* 232).

For Beebe, the return to New York, to his apartment on Central Park West and his association with his many friends in the theater, fostered a lifestyle that could be thought of as Bohemian. Friends met at a nearby establishment called the

Hotel des Artists, a place where actors, actresses, writers, and musicians gathered. While Beebe was in the South Pacific, he loaned his apartment to Elswyth Thane, a novelist with several books published. The relationship grew when Beebe returned in July of 1925 and he and Elswyth were married in 1927. Their social life enhanced Beebe's love for theater and music and included friendships with people like Katharine Hepburn, Douglas Fairbanks, Will Rogers and Jascha Heifetz, as well as people who were eager to provide money for his research which continued nonstop. At that moment, Beebe was still working to organize and identify specimens brought back from the *Arcturus* exploration.

Honeymooning in Bermuda for a couple of months and finding a rich social life there as well, Beebe became interested in Nonsuch Island, a small island off the coast where the ocean dropped off to depths of a half mile and more. When it became known that Beebe had plans to continue his research there, the new adventure was sponsored by two of his oldest patrons and friends, Harrison Williams and Mortimer Schiff.

The plan was to research an eight-mile cylinder off Nonsuch with the use of a modified helmet, trawls and nets. But in November of 1928 a story in *The New York Times* described Beebe's intention to continue underwater exploration in some sort of device that would allow him to explore deep-sea creatures in their habitat. Beebe's plan was not only to descend to lower depths, but to observe sea life in the context of their environment that previously had been brought up by the trawls. He was also eager to explore the ocean floor and the contours of the volcano that had formed Bermuda.

Because of *The New York Times* article, Beebe was bombarded by hopeful engineers touting all sorts of designs for a vehicle that could withstand the pressure of deep-sea diving. Through the centuries, attempts to design equipment such as this all ended in failure. This time, however, there was a young engineer, Otis Barton, who appeared on the horizon and who was at first ignored by Beebe. Barton, an admirer of Beebe's, was studying to be a naturalist scientist at Columbia University. A friend managed to arrange a meeting between Barton and Beebe during which the possibility of a sphere was discussed. The idea of some sort of submersible began long ago in talks at Sagamore Hill with Teddy Roosevelt, who had suggested the submersible should be a sphere. The cylinder drawn by Beebe had a flat surface at the top and bottom and was soon ruled out. Flat surfaces a half mile down would collapse in deep-sea pressure with the weight of half a ton on each square inch. The entire surface of a sphere would withstand pressure equally.

The steel sphere was being cast in New Jersey, and while Barton tended to the problems that arose with its manufacture, Beebe and his staff were converting the old buildings on Nonsuch Island into a research laboratory and a residence for the team. In the Depression years of 1930 and 1931, money was scarce, but due to the generosity of the Rockefeller Foundation and the New York Zoological Association, Beebe was able to continue with his plans. In the meantime, he began going out to sea off the coast of Nonsuch with a trawler every morning to set out nets that often went a mile down. Evenings were spent classifying the catch.

When the sphere arrived from New Jersey, it was soon discovered that even the largest winch and reels taken from the *Arcturus* could not handle its five-ton bulk on the deck of the current vessel, the *Ready.* So back to New Jersey it went to be recast. This time, the weight was reduced to 5,400 pounds. It was now referred to as the bathysphere, *bathy* from Greek meaning deep. The walls were an inch and a half thick. The three-inch-thick windows were made of clear fused quartz. Clarity was important to Beebe because he was eager to know the rate at which the levels of light fall off as the sphere descended. Light was important to understanding the type of fish that lived in dark environments.

The fifty-four-inch diameter interior of the sphere had no floor and was painted black inside and the exterior, white. The bathysphere was connected to a non-twisting cable 3,500 feet long that weighed two tons. It had to be handled carefully as the bathysphere descended into the sea. Inside the bathysphere were telephone, light wires, and an oxygen cable. There were tanks containing two liters of oxygen, wire racks containing calcium chloride for absorbing moisture, and soda lime for removing excess carbon dioxide.

The place chosen for the first descent was about eight miles off the coast of Nonsuch where the depth of the ocean was about one mile. On May 27, 1930, the first submersion took place.

> *Finally, we were all ready and I looked around at the sea and sky, the boats and my friends, and not being able to think of any pithy saying which might echo down the ages, I said nothing, crawled painfully*

> *over the steel bolts, fell inside and curled up on the cold, hard bottom of the sphere* (*Remarkable Life* 285*)*.

After Beebe and Barton crawled into the bathysphere, the four-hundred-pound hatch was hammered into place and secured by heavy bolts. On the day of that first test, the bathysphere was lifted, swung over the side of the *Ready,* and lowered into the water to a depth of forty-five feet. During this test, the interior of the bathysphere remained dry except for some condensation. It was definitely cause for tepid celebration.

On the second dive of seven-hundred feet, the disappearance of light became apparent. Beebe notes that a description had to be a dichotomy of words, calling it *a strange brilliance of darkness.* The spectroscope showed that red was the first wavelength to disappear, then orange, yellow, then green. At eight hundred feet, there was nothing but a faint tinge of violet and at two thousand feet every trace of light disappeared. What remained was *an indefinable translucent blue quite unlike anything I have ever seen in the upper world. (The Remarkable Life of William Beebe*, pg. 289). As they descended further there was the terrible slow change from dark blue to blacker blue, a view that was *the most impressive thing about the descent.*

Beebe had seen fish from this level as they were pulled up in the nets, but since those fish had not survived, this was the first time he was able to see them active in their environment and in their iridescence. Here there were shrimp, flying snails, jellyfish, and fish that were so transparent only their stomach contents were visible. As the bathysphere descended to deeper levels, Beebe was surprised at the size of sea life, as it was always assumed the fish in deeper depths were large. This was not the case. Also, the number of sea specimens caught in the nets did not represent the enormous abundance of creatures in the lower depths. That was apparent now. There was sea life that was blind, that carried high iridescence and long feelers to make up for the lack of sight, and had very large mouths and large teeth or fangs, and stomachs that had the ability to extend to a size much larger than their original bodies. It was eat or be eaten and it was a completely carnivorous affair.

On the fifth day of diving, June 11, the bathysphere descended to a depth of over a quarter of a mile, 1,426 feet. As light diminished, Beebe saw a lanternfish (*Myctophids*) lit up for the first time: *fish that were ablaze with their full armor of iridescence.* There followed descriptions of many different kinds of fish and crustaceans, but it was the first sighting of the lanternfish with a tentacle that reached over its head with a light at the end of it, and the living silver (*Argyropelecus*) hatchet fish with its bulging eyes, that most thrilled Beebe. First seen, Beebe noted that there were *groups of lights moving along slowly, or jerking unsteadily past, and the searing beams of the searchlight revealed these as silver hatchetfish, gleaming with tinsel, but with every light quenched, at least to my vision, until I switched off the electricity ...* (*National Geographic*, June, 1931, 666). Seen in the absolute darkness of the deep sea, these drifters were illuminated by small groups of many-colored lights over their entire body. The eyes were elongated and telescopic, useful in the utter darkness. There were luminated squid with lights along their tentacles and swivel-toothed dragon fish in pursuit of them.

About the experience of descending a quarter of a mile, Beebe writes,

> *I pressed my face against the glass and looked upward and in the slight segment which I could manage I saw a faint paling of the blue. I peered down and again I felt the old longing to go farther, although it looked like the black pit-mouth of hell itself—yet it still showed blue. My window was clear as crystal, in fact clearer, for fused quartz is one of the most transparent of all substances and transmits all wavelengths of sunlight. The outside world I now saw through it was, however, a solid blue-black world, one which seemed born of a single vibration—blue, blue, forever and forever blue* (*National Geographic*, June 1931, 675).

> *There came to me at that instant a tremendous wave of emotion, a real appreciation of what was momentarily almost superhuman, cosmic, of the whole situation; our barge slowly rolling high overhead in the blazing sunlight, like the merest chip in the midst of the ocean, the long cobweb of cable leading down through the spectrum to our lonely sphere, where, sealed tight, two conscious human beings sat*

> *and peered into the abysmal darkness as we dangled in mid-water, isolated as a lost planet in outermost space (National Geographic, June 1931, 678).*

The importance of art in rendering live fish in their habitat cannot be underestimated. As Beebe described what he was seeing to Gloria Hollister, the person at the other end of the telephone line recording Beebe's descriptions on the *Ready*, Else Bostelmann, a nature artist, was able to render what was described to her with great accuracy. The results of her recording were proven years later by advances in photography. These beautiful paintings appeared in several issues of *National Geographic* in 1931 and 1932. As a result, the public was tuned in to every aspect of the research.

The diversity of sea life is challenging to record here. At eight hundred feet there were clouds of copepods. Silvery squid shot past and lantern fish were in abundance, even fish that were found at higher levels. When they reached a thousand feet, the inside of the bathysphere remained dry. They traveled through clouds of flying snails and shrimps. They saw an anglerfish, whose features included a lemon-colored light on its overhead tentacle and rows of glowing sinister teeth. At two thousand feet, two long black sea eels and a sea dragon-like fish passed by the window. All in all, Beebe noted what was brought up in the nets was a *great underrepresentation of the density of sea life.*

When they made their deepest dive at 3,028 feet, the half-mile mark was celebrated with blasts from the *Ready* high above them and resounding announcements from the press, including several mentions in *The National Geographic* articles. At this depth, Beebe noted they had descended into a world that was solid blue-black. Beebe carefully wiped the glass window and felt his body pressed more heavily against the floor. He began to realize a frustration at the fewer number of sea creatures at this level and became aware of the too-narrow window, which was about as large as his face. However, to go any lower at this time did not seem to be the safest thing to do. What he had already seen he later described as feeling like *an astronomer might who looks through his telescope after having rocketed to Mars and back, or like a paleontologist who could suddenly annihilate time and see his fossils alive (National Geographic, June 1931, 675).*

After the dives in the bathysphere in 1932, Putnam published Beebe's book, *Nonsuch, Land of Water*, a dissertation on the history of the island and appreciation of its geology and especially of its coral reefs. He writes, *If only people would only look, if we would only see what is before us, if we would just change our egocentric perspectives, the world would be a finer place.* To that end, Beebe consented to an event that was an unusual happening at that time.

In 1932, NBC wanted to have a half-hour broadcast from the bathysphere with Beebe explaining what he was seeing. Beebe's words traveled through the telephone cable, to a transmitter on Bermuda, sent to AT&T in New Jersey, on to New York where they were transmitted across the U.S. and even to the BBC in England. The public was invited to experience what a half hour of a deep-sea dive was like. Beebe shared his experiences generously in several different ways. All of it helped in the constant search for funding as the effects of the Depression became all encompassing, until finally the bathysphere dives had to be abandoned for the season in 1933. The bathysphere spent that year in Chicago, on loan to the American Museum for an exhibit on underwater exploration.

Hopes for further dives by Beebe and the bathysphere were kept alive by *The National Geographic* in 1934. The now four-year-old sphere, when sent back to New Jersey for refurbishing, revealed a number of flaws and small fractures that had to be taken care of. When completed, the sphere was sent to Bermuda where plans for more dives were in the works. The latest dive took place in August of that year. In all, sixteen deep sea dives over three seasons were made in addition to dives that studied the contour of the ocean floor and the coral reefs. These dives proved to be more dangerous than the deep-sea adventures as at one point, the bathysphere nearly hit a coral reef due to the unevenness and unpredictability of the bottom, as well as its inability to maneuver in any direction. The addition of two platforms at the base of the bathysphere were installed to stabilize it in landings among the nooks and crannies of the reef.

THE HALF-MILE DESCENT BECAME the name of Beebe's latest book as well as a comprehensive article with the same title in *The National Geographic, Half Mile Down.* Will missed none of it. His obsession to keep tabs on a man he admired and understood was constant throughout his life. He found pictures in *The National Geographic* of Beebe on his hands and knees crawling out of the bathysphere as if to say, "there's no way to do this gracefully." Then there was in a later issue, a photo of Beebe, looking serious in a suit and tie, overcoat and hat, standing next to the battered exterior and peeling paint of the old bathysphere which had been placed outdoors at the New York Aquarium. Writer and friend Ruth Rose stands next to him in business attire. Both look very serious, as though detached from the magnificent ball of steel beside them. There seems to be no connection between those two formally dressed humans dressed in winter clothes, standing outdoors next to a structure of peeling paint and obvious neglect, to the remembrance of sunny days in tropical heat, wearing shorts, canvas shoes, and sunhats, smiling at each new discovery.

In 1961 or thereabouts, Will brought the family to see the bathysphere where it was exhibited on Coney Island, New York. It was a first, now apparently on display with little general acknowledgment of what had taken place in 1932. Yet it is among the first memories he has of Beebe coming out of the ocean and landing on the deck of the Arcturus with *sargassum* weed hanging off his arms and laughing, that brings a smile to Will's face these forty years later; Beebe hanging on to the side of the lifeboat waiting to have the helmet removed from his shoulders; Beebe pouring over the basins of minute sea life after a good haul. It was a humble beginning to deep-sea research, but significant. In the end, every step forward was significant in establishing Beebe's role not only in the study of oceanography but in many other areas of evolution in animals, insects, and birds.

Beebe was an open door to life. The bathysphere, now a remnant along the path of a dedicated man, has been exceeded by the modern technology of unmanned vehicles for deep sea exploration directed on board ship by computers, or human occupied submersibles and automated towed robots. Still, honor must be given to the man who laid the foundation and dared to be the first to enter that very blue-black world.

The transition from the Victorian era of collect and classify to the expansion of the study of the interrelationships of organisms and their environment was begun by Theodore Roosevelt and William Beebe. Their collaboration pushed forward the idea of the necessity of research in habitat and had changed the direction of oceanography as well as that of entomology and tropical ecology. Beebe's focus on proving Darwinian theories was carried on in new ways in varying settings such as the Galapagos, the ocean cylinders of Nonsuch in the Atlantic, and Station 74 in the Pacific.

Beebe went further in his research than had ever been accomplished before. In discovering new species through his intense carefulness and imagination, his influence on scientists ever since has been enormous and the bravery of his descent into the unknown a beginning in the study of the oceans.

Many of the scientists who worked with Beebe at different times went on to foster conservation, among them Rachel Carlson, author of *Silent Spring*; Gloria Hollister, whose work led to the establishment of The Nature Conservancy and the establishment of the Wildlife Conservation Society; as well as the work of Jacques Cousteau in oceanography.

The case for evolution is ever-present in Beebe's work. As the *Arcturus* headed for the New York Harbor in July of 1925, the Scopes Trial was taking place in Tennessee with arguments for and against scientific evidence. Beebe's work continually stated the case for evolution.

> *As my line stretches back my brain contracts, my muscles expand, I drop down on all fours, sprout a tail, develop long ears and snout, my teeth simplify and insects satisfy my hunger, reptilian characters accrue, my ribs increase; I slip into the water, and looking for the last time upon the land, I sink beneath the surface. Gills mark my rhythm of breath, limbs shrink to fins, and even these vanish, while my backbone, last hold upon the higher life, dissolves to a notochord. At one end of my evolution Roosevelt called me friend—millions of years earlier any passing worm might have hailed me as brother (Nonsuch-Land of Water* 313-314*).*

Light's Mysteries

October now, the streetlights brighten on 85th Road. Everyone on the block is home from work and having dinner. Light is different for him, makes him proud and humble, too, because of what he'd seen as if a light was turned on inside of him. The volcano was still speaking to him, the fire and the sunset sky that lasted through the night and then the appearance of the shooting star. In the end, it is all about light, the many different kinds that draw humanity to it.

But it is about turbulence, too, and its necessity in the beginning of anything. Could the same be said about war? Did anyone believe good could come out of chaos? Maybe.

On a hot night he stood on the deck of the *Arcturus,* arms leaning on the rail, waiting. He saw it a few times before but thought it was the fingernail moon's light shining on the water or something that had fallen from the sky. *Not real*, he remembered thinking. It only happened when the sun was going down and light from above disappeared, turning the world into night, as if it were only an illusion. He had stared into the water and at the surface water beyond. The moon hung where it belonged, telling nothing. He blinked again and again. Whatever it was stayed there, but moved, too. Something living, floating, a collective motion, against the will of the water. Just there. He swore it could only be his imagination.

Yet, Beebe stared, too, on those nights when he stood with his head bent over the railing of the deck. It was an image of him that Will never forgot. Even when everyone else had retired after a day of extensive use of the nets and all they had brought up from the deep, there stood Beebe, staring into the water, just a few feet away from him, never noticing him, his full attention on the water below, tired from all the work of the day, yet discovering one more opportunity to find out. Beebe saw the light, too.

Last summer, when Will was out fishing in a rented boat in Sheepshead Bay, Long Island, he was coming in as night darkened. He again saw the light on or in or under the water. Why the sight should thrill him he didn't know, but it connected him to the night he and Herr Beebe stood at the rail at the same time, although Beebe wasn't aware of his presence. Beebe's curiosity impressed him as a kid. For many things there are no answers, but Herr Beebe discovered answers and shared them with the public, which is what made him so unique, popularizing that encompassing mystery of ocean.

Fragments, *motes,* as Beebe called them, weren't seen in daylight. They floated near the surface of the water but they could not be detected until dark, and then the population that floated lit up, surrounding the ship with the miracle of stardust as he thought of it then. He remembers watching for a while until the need for sleep overcame him and he returned to his bunk. The next several nights, he watched again and again. What was it?

The answer came a generation or two later, the words lifting off the page. For Beebe, every bit of life was to be considered and detailed. It was plankton, floating oceanic life composed of myriad motes described as phosphorescent, the new word. Whale food. But the investigation went deeper, of course. Beebe took samples. He went beyond what he could observe at first sight. With amazing thoroughness, every bit of sea life was analyzed and counted with the census revealing both animal and plant life that was not only food for whales, but a whole sequence of life serving phenomena even as far as the humans at the end of the chain. Beebe claimed that men lost at sea without food could fashion a scoop out of a shirt and dragging it overboard could catch enough food for dinner, at least enough to ward off devastating starvation. Appealing it was not, but the intent was to show how the ocean could sustain mankind and everything that lives.

As for Will, he had only watched in silence and was limited, lacking the words to understand what others were saying. But Beebe, with his dedication to science and his inexhaustible focus and acceptance of what he found and put into words with feeling and clarity, was the light that lent reality to what Will observed in those six months of his sixteenth year and again now as the streetlights brighten 85th Road.

There was nothing harsh about Beebe. It was Beebe's love of life that commanded respect. There was no fear, no guilt in Beebe's example. His was a life spent searching for knowledge, for truth, where the exciting part of gaining knowledge was the surprise of discovery. And for this, Beebe took leaps of faith and daring. The miracle was that he wrote it all down and shared it and in so doing, fostered interest and serious research in the ocean worldwide. It was the greatest unexplored world within man's reach to pioneer at the time. And here are the words that reached across the years for which Will, staring at the streetlight outside the window, is grateful.

It was not enough to count the sea life contained in a drop of water, a strenuous undertaking that led to a number. Beebe had poured the jar of water into a tray. In the light there was no trace of luminescence, so he turned it off, and then saw a tray full of diamonds. *Sapphirina*, copepods, an eighth of an inch long, minute marine crustaceans and *Sagitta*, wormlike in structure, and *Cyclops*, a crustacean with one eye, two antennae and a color range from red to deep blue, so piliferous they came in numbers of thirty million in many plankton hauls. It could be said these creatures could correspond to the numbers of insects on land. Some of those creatures had appendages to help with buoyancy, but curiously, they also had the quality of transparency. Sometimes the only way they could be detected was by the evidence of the food they'd eaten.

There was one more item of note, the story of

> *Phyllosoma — a creature who cast no more shadow than the thinnest skim of clear ice. Yet it was a living animal, more than three inches long, with all the general organs which we ourselves possess—eyes, mouth, feet, stomach, nerves, muscles, and a strong will to live (Arcturus* 210*).*

These creatures were virtually helpless, drifting along by the power of current and wind. Trying to number them was like counting the kernels of sand on a beach.

> *... we poured out an overflowing mass of rich pink jelly into a white flat tray. This I weighed carefully and then took, as exactly as possible, a one-hundred-and-fiftieth portion. I began to go over this but soon became discouraged, and again divided it and set to work on one sixth of the fraction on which I had first started. After many hours of eye-straining and counting under the microscope, I conservatively estimated my 1/150 part of the hour's plankton haul as follows:*

Feathery copepods— Candace-like, 7,920;
Bright blue copepods — Pontella-like, 71,400;
Other copepods— Canalus-like, pink, 139,320;
Bivalve crustacea — Ostracod-like, 4,920;
Short-eyed shrimps, 720;
Siphonophores, 4,400;
Helix snails, 8,880;
Purple Ianthina snails , 13,440;
Egg masses of snails , 1,080;
Free eggs, various, 5,280;
Arrow-like flying snails, 2,520;
Nautilus-like flying snails, 240;
Oyster-like flying snails, 960.

> *If we multiply this by one hundred and fifty we get forty million, six hundred and sixty-two thousand individuals. Please remember that this is a very conservative estimate of only a few of the more easily counted groups in one small haul of an hour's duration, and the magnitude of the life of the sea will begin to dawn upon our minds* (*Arcturus* 199-200).

Astonished, Will reads those words again and again. The word *plankton* comes from the Greek and means *wanderer*. The movement of its creatures is propelled by wind and current as the life within it has no means of propelling itself, making it easy dining for fish. And then they, of course, are attacked in turn by middle-sized fish only to be consumed by larger ones, who, in dying, supply food for other species as well. Plankton then could be said to be the beginning of the circle of life.

Herr Beebe had lowered the jar into the water that night when the sea lit up, reaching to discover the very depths of the puzzle.

There was another new word. Bioluminescence: the emission of light from living organisms. What would it be called when the light came from a man? Explorer, teacher, writer, scientist, pioneer? Musician? Herr Beebe was all of those.

Will clears his throat. The sound reminds him where he is, in Bellerose, living securely in a long-awaited and hard-earned home. It was so long ago now. Over forty years. The memory of his first job is still as fresh as every early morning when he had once called out *Half pass six* in the hours, days, and months of his awakening.

Acknowledgments

My utmost gratitude to Ron Sauder, editor of Secant Publishing, for the publication of this one-hundred-year-old story that has been on my mind for countless years. His interest, support, wisdom, and patience in large doses have brought these pages to the light of day, for which there is no thank you large enough.

To family and friends who read the manuscript and offered suggestions and criticism, I thank you for your encouragement and words of insight.

And in memory of Robert Wright, friend and fellow teacher, who long ago gave me three copies of *National Geographic Magazine* from his vast collection, which sat on my bookshelf for years. I thank you for that ever-present reminder to tell the story of Beebe and a bit of family history. Robert, I finally got to it.

Bibliography

William Beebe, *The Arcturus Adventure*, G. P. Putnam's Sons (1926), The Knickerbocker Press, New York and London.

William Beebe, *Jungle Days*, Garden City Publishing Co., Inc. (1923), New York.

William Beebe, *Beneath Tropical Seas*, Blue Ribbon Books (1928), New York.

William Beebe, "A Round Trip to Davy Jones Locker," *National Geographic Magazine*, National Geographic Society, June 1931.

William Beebe, "The Depths of the Sea," *National Geographic Magazine*, National Geographic Society, January 1932.

William Beebe, "A Wanderer Under the Sea," *National Geographic Magazine*, National Geographic Society, December 1932.

William Beebe, "Beebe Gathers Marine Wonders," *The New York Times*, June 7, 1925.

Carol Grant Gould, *The Remarkable Life of William Beebe, Explorer and Naturalist,* Island Press (2004).

David Binney Putnam, *David Goes Voyaging*, G. P. Putnam's Sons (1925), The Knickerbocker Press.

About the Author

A native of New York City, Barbara Lockhart lives on a farm on the Eastern Shore of Maryland. She is the recipient of two Individual Artist Awards in Fiction from the Maryland State Arts Council for her short stories and her first novel, *Requiem for a Summer Cottage* as well as a silver medal from the Independent Book Publishers Awards for her historical novel, *Elizabeth's Field*. She has authored and co-authored four children's books and a nationwide program for the teaching of children's literature, *Read to me, Talk with me.* Her short stories have appeared in such venues as *Indiana Review*, *The Greensboro Review* and *Pleiades*.